CADOGAN guides

perfect honeymoons
& original weddings
summer

The Dream Destination	1
The Ideal Hotel	7
Honeymoon Hot-spots	17
Alternative Weddings	157
Alternative Honeymoons	163

Cadogan Books plc
London House, Parkgate Road,
London SW11 4NQ, UK
Distributed in the USA by
The Globe Pequot Press
6 Business Park Road, PO Box 833, Old Saybrook,
Connecticut 06475-0833

Copyright © Louise Roddon 1995
Illustrations © Charles Shearer 1995
Cover illustrations by Horatio Monteverde

Book and cover design by Animage
Series Editors: Rachel Fielding and Vicki Ingle
Additional Material: Mary Douglas
Editing and Proofreading: Vicki Ingle,
  Katrina Burroughs, Linda McQueen
DTP and Design: Kicca Tommasi
Production: Rupert Wheeler Book Production Services

All rights reserved. No part of this publication may be reproduced, stored in a retrieval system, or transmitted, in any form or by any means, electronic or mechanical, including photocopying and recording, or by any information storage and retrieval system except as may be expressly permitted by the UK 1988 Copyright Design & Patents Act and the USA 1976 Copyright Act or in writing from the publisher. Requests for permission should be addressed to Cadogan Books plc, London House, Parkgate Road, London SW11 4NQ.

A catalogue record for this book is available from the British Library
ISBN 1-86011-001-0

Output by Bookworm, Manchester
Printed and bound in the UK by Redwood Books, Trowbridge, Wiltshire

The author and publishers have made every effort to ensure the accuracy of the information in the book at the time of going to press. However, they cannot accept any responsibility for any loss, injury or inconvenience resulting from the use of information contained in this guide.

About the Author

Louise Roddon was the travel editor of *You and Your Wedding* so her experience of the honeymoon market is not only extensive but exhaustive. She also writes on every aspect of nuptial, health and travel matters for newspapers and magazines such as the *European*, *The Times*, *Today*, *Here's Health* and *Burke's Peerage*. She is an executive editor of *Caribbean Life* and has twice won the Mexican government travel writing award, '*La Pluma de Plata*'.

Acknowledgements

My thanks go to all brides and grooms for their honeymooning anecdotes, warnings and recommendations. I'd also like to thank: Penny Brook, Fiona Cameron; Vicki, Katrina and Linda at Cadogan; all those tourism representatives who helped me in compiling this guide; and my husband David for acting as the perfect groom.

Please help us keep this guide up to date

Although the information in this guide was correct at the time of printing, practical details such as opening hours, travel information, standards in hotels and restaurants and, in particular, prices are liable to change.

We would be delighted to receive any comments concerning exisiting entries or omissions. Significant contributions will be acknowledged in the next edition, and authors of the best letters will receive a copy of the Cadogan Guide of their choice.

Contents

Guide to the Guide vi

The Dream Destination — 1–6

Making the Decisions	2	Specialist Tour Operators	5
Some Important Dos and Don'ts	33		

The Ideal Hotel — 7–16

The Ingredients of a Romantic Hotel	8	Pampering the Bride-to-be	13
Adding Up the Cost	10	UK Spa Trek	14
The Perfect Preparation	12	US Spa Trek	15

Honeymoon Hot-spots 17–156

Introduction	17	Greek Islands	81
Destination Finder	18	Ireland: County Clare	91
Bali	19	Italy: Florence	97
England: Cumbria	29	Italy: Portofino	103
England: Devon	35	Italy: Positano	109
England: Dorset	41	Jersey: St Saviour	115
England: Sussex	47	Portugal: The Algarve	121
Fiji	53	Scotland: Dunkeld	127
France: Côte d'Azur	63	The Seychelles	133
France: Paris	69	South Africa: *Blue Train*	145
France: Le Touquet	75	USA: San Francisco	151

Alternative Weddings 157–162

Love in a Strange Climate	158	Specialist Tour Operators	162
How and Where to Wed	159	Original Options in the UK	162
Wacky Weddings	160		
What to Wear	161		

Alternative Honeymoons 163–168

Sporty Honeymoons	164	Spiritual Honeymoons	166
Big Adventure Honeymoons	165	Budget Honeymoons	166

Contents

Guide to the Guide

This book aims to help you and your spouse-to-be choose the perfect location for your dream honeymoon. The first two chapters, **The Dream Destination** and **The Ideal Hotel**, guide you in a general way through some decision-making processes and should help you to narrow down your choices. Following this is **Honeymoon Hot-spots**, a selection of 25 specific recommendations for perfect honeymoons worldwide. Organised alphabetically by country, these suggestions may be followed in detail or used as inspiration for developing your own ideas. **Alternative Weddings** covers possibilities for actually marrying abroad, at your honeymoon destination or in various other unusual settings; finally, **Alternative Honeymoons** gives a list of suggestions for those in a sporty, adventurous, spiritual or thrifty as well as romantic mood.

| Making the Decisions | 2 |

The Dream Destination

| Some Important Dos and Don'ts | 3 |
| Specialist Tour Operators | 5 |

Your betrothed fancies white-water rafting along the Zambezi; you, on the other hand, favour a tropical paradise of palm trees, piña coladas and white sandy beaches. One of the first surprises of life-long partnership is the discovery that your beloved has some tastes that are entirely different from your own. During the early stages of a relationship these differences are often concealed, and sometimes a wedding can be a couple's the first real source of conflict.

But there's no reason for differing tastes to cause disagreements. Compromise is the key: this is not the right arena for a battle of wills. Sit down and discuss exactly what you both want from the trip. Draw up a shortlist of points and work out a budget, not forgetting to allow for a few hidden extras that will really make it the holiday of a lifetime.

If you are planning a surprise honeymoon, amass as much information as possible on what you both enjoy before booking—that way you can still keep the honeymoon a romantic secret, but reduce the risk of making a disappointing and expensive mistake.

Making the Decisions

- Do you want a hot or cold **climate**? Remember that muggy tropical climes can affect your mood, temper, and even your energy levels.

- How much **time** do you have? If you want a honeymoon in a faraway location, remember that long, tiring journeys can be a source of stress.

- Do you want the **buzz** of a city holiday or prefer something more peaceful?

- Would you enjoy the traditional **beach** honeymoon? If so, does the **sand** have to be powder-white? Some resorts are based on volcanic islands where the beach is composed of black sand or rocks and pebbles instead.

- If your honeymoon is going to last a fortnight or more, then a totally beach-based destination might begin to pall after a week or ten days. Discuss whether you would like a resort near some **sights** of interest or with access to **ethnic culture**. Would you like to take part in **sports** or **day trips**?

- Is cuisine important? Do you prefer **ethnic** or more **international** food?

The Dream Destination

One groom insisted on planning a surprise, and his wife-to-be went along with it, convinced he had picked up her hints of far-off oceans and deserted bays. She duly packed lots of bikinis and T-shirts, only to find herself in cold and rainy Alaska. Brides may like surprises, but only if you get it right!

- Is a good comfortable **hotel** all important (*see* 'The Ideal Hotel', pp.7–16)? Do you want the **full honeymoon treatment** (champagne, flowers, lots of silly jokes from tour reps), or do you prefer something more discreet?
- Can either of you speak the **language**? If some far-flung destination appeals, how will you communicate?

If your initial discussions seem to be taking you in completely opposite directions, don't panic. Disparate preferences can be satisfied by a **two-centre** honeymoon: an exciting week on an African safari, for example, would combine perfectly with a lazy spell at an Indian Ocean beach resort. Even in a single location, a compromise can be made between rest and activity: a private island in the Seychelles may look as though it can offer little more than lazing about in hammocks, but there will be opportunities for the restless spouse to attempt some exciting deep-sea fishing or snorkelling, to go island-hopping, or to learn to sail or dive.

Some Important Dos and Don'ts

- ✔ **Do** keep an open mind and look at as many brochures as possible. Ask your well-travelled friends and family for their recommendations. You might like to try somewhere that neither of you would normally consider.
- ✔ **Do** work out a **budget**, however unromantic this may sound, allowing for lots of hidden extras.
- ✘ **Don't** spring a total surprise on your bride-to-be—at least not without a few very clear hints being swapped along the way.
- ✔ **Do** contact a number of travel agents until you find one who has detailed knowledge of hotel properties, local amenities, climate, even the general culture and cost of living at the destination. The money a good agent saves you can buy a bottle of champagne, a meal or even a room upgrade. For a list of reliable tour operators with honeymoon expertise, *see* pp.5–6.

✗ **Don't** be fooled by brochurespeak and glossy photographs. Pictures will generally feature only the best room in the hotel, and may conceal a hideous building site opposite. Make sure you ask your operator about the hotel's position, its accessibility to the beach or other attractions, whether a double bed is guaranteed, and anything else that's important to you.

✔ **Do** ask your travel agent whether **sports** and **activities** are included. Many good resort hotels in places like the Caribbean, Fiji and the Seychelles include tennis, waterskiing, snorkelling, canoeing, windsurfing. Diving, deep-sea fishing, sailing and organised excursions tend to cost extra. It might pay to contact the local tourist office for a list of sights and guides.

✗ **Don't** go to places one of you has visited before, especially with a former love. The 'before you met me' syndrome can really grate if the conversation is peppered with comments like, 'Sarah and I had a fabulous lunch there,' or, 'I recognise that waiter from when I was here with Paul...'

✗ **Don't** travel on the same day as your wedding, if at all possible. If you are flying off somewhere, pick a pretty hotel near the airport, unwind after the reception and get an early night if you can. You will arrive at your honeymoon destination wonderfully refreshed, rather than jaded and hung-over.

✔ **Do** take a camera and loads of film. You will probably want to gloat over your honeymoon photos for many months after the event—even if you risk boring the pants off your friends.

✗ **Don't** raise your romantic expectations. During the wedding, there will be pressure to be happy and lovey-dovey, yet you may start your honeymoon with a huge row. Don't despair. You will not be the first—often the sheer strain of the wedding preparations precipitates the row. Take it easy. Don't expect to feel romantic or indeed sexy all the time. Expect a few disappointments, then the pleasant surprises will be all the more memorable.

✔ **Do** apply for a **credit card**, if you don't already have one. They can be lifesavers in a foreign country. Likewise, try to obtain some local **currency** in small bills before you travel; this will be useful for drinks, telephone calls, tipping and taxis.

After discussing what you both want, you should be able to settle on a type of holiday (beach, city, rural) and a suitable climate. Once you have chosen your resort, you are ready to begin your search for the ideal hotel.

Specialist Tour Operators

The Best of Greece, 5th Floor, 23–24 Margaret Street, London W1N 8LE, ✆ (0171) 255 2320.

British Virgin Islands Club, 66 High Street, Walton-on-Thames, Surrey KT12 1BU, ✆ (01932) 247 617.

Citalia, Marco Polo House, 305 Landsowne Rd, Croydon, Surrey CR9 1LL, ✆ (0235) 824 354, ✆ (0181) 686 5533.

Corfu à la Carte, The White House, Bucklebury Alley, Cold Ash, Newbury, Berkshire RG16 9NN, ✆ (01635) 201 140.

Inspirations, Victoria House, Victoria Road, Horley, Surrey RH6 7AD, ✆ (01293) 820 207.

CV Travel's Different World of Hotels, 43 Cadogan Street, London SW3 2PR ✆ (0171) 581 0851.

French Expressions/Italian Expressions, 13 McCrone Mews, Belsize Lane, London NW3 5BG, ✆ (0171) 794 1480.

Greek Islands Club, 66 High Street, Walton-on-Thames, Surrey KT12 1BU ✆ (01932) 220 477.

Kirker Holidays, 3 New Concordia Wharf, Mill Street, London SE1 2BB, ✆ (0171) 231 3333.

Magic of Italy, 227 Shepherds Bush Road, London W6 7AS, ✆ (0303) 226 670; ✆ (0181) 748 7575.

Passage to South America, 113 Shepherds Bush Road, London W6 7LP ✆ (0171) 602 94889.

Prestige Holidays, 14 Market Place, Ringwood, Hampshire BH24 1JA.

Silverbird, 'The Far East Travel Specialists', 4 Northfields Prospect, Putney Bridge Road, London SW18 1PE, ✆ (0181) 875 9090.

Somak Holidays, Somak House, Harrovian Village, Bessborough Road, Harrow on the Hill, Middlesex HA1 3EX, ✆ (0181) 423 3000.

Tropical Places, Freshfield House, Lewes Road, Forest Row, West Sussex RH18 5ES, ✆ (01342) 825 599/825 123.

Unicorn Holidays Ltd., The Best of France, Mallorca, Spain & Portugal, 2 Place Farm, Wheathampstead, Hertfordshire AL4 8SB, ✆ (01582) 834 400.

Two pensioners decided that an off-season break in Venice would make an ideal honeymoon. Arriving at their hotel in the afternoon, they settled in, had a wonderful dinner and then went out for a moonlit stroll. Unfortunately they soon became lost. 'I didn't want to cause alarm,' said the groom later, 'so for the first hour I pretended I knew where we were going. I thought we'd just walk along the canal.' Eventually they stopped a policeman to ask directions—only to realise they couldn't remember the name of their hotel. By now it was approaching midnight. Local officials phoned likely hotels, but without success, and finally the couple were taken to a less than romantic guesthouse. At dawn, the groom drew back the curtain and looked out—only to see their hotel, on the opposite side of the canal...

The Ingredients of a Romantic Hotel	8
Adding Up the Cost	10
The Perfect Preparation	12
Pampering the Bride-to-be	13

The Ideal Hotel

A favourably positioned hotel with attractive bedrooms and a friendly atmosphere should be a honeymoon priority. If you are planning a tropical honeymoon, your hotel will be a retreat from the heat of the day—ideally you should book a decent-sized bedroom with a private balcony, a well-equipped bathroom, and a ceiling fan or air-conditioning. Similarly, if you are travelling to a cooler climate, your hotel will be a cosy haven after a day's sightseeing.

The Ingredients of a Romantic Hotel

A Beautiful Setting

Choose somewhere by a lake, in lovely gardens or a forest, overlooking a private stretch of coast or near some famous landmarks. Hotels in outstandingly lovely settings include: Burgh Island (Devon), Gravetye Manor (West Sussex), Sharrow Bay (Cumbria), Biras Creek (Virgin Gorda, British Virgin Islands), Hotel Splendido (Portofino, Italy), Le Sirenuse (Positano, Italy), Villa Argentikon (Chios, Greece), Lake Palace Hotel (Udaipur, India), Copacabana Palace (Rio de Janeiro), the Datai (Langkawi, Malaysia).

A Room with a View

Try the Marquis Suite, Glitter Bay (Barbados), Sharrow Bay (Lake Ullswater, Cumbria), the Mandarin Oriental (San Francisco), the Four Seasons (Bali), Tsitouras Collection (Santorini, Greece), Villa San Michele (Florence), the Savoy (London).

Sheer Luxury

It is better to have 5 nights in a rather expensive hotel where the staff treat you like royalty than 10 nights of surly service, poor plumbing and an uncomfortable bed. Reliable groups include Leading Hotels of the World, Orient-Express Hotels and Relais & Châteaux (individual hotels, often with owner–managers, run by the 'rule of the five Cs': Character, Courtesy, Calm, Charm and Cuisine).

The danger with booking a honeymoon is that we tend to use our hearts rather than our heads. One couple picked Paris for its tradition for romance. They invested all they had in a week's low-season package at a top-class hotel during the month of February. Since the deal was for bed and breakfast, and the hotel turned out to be too intimidating to encourage lounging about in the public rooms, they spent a wet and miserable 7 days tramping the streets in search of warmth and somewhere cheap to eat. It was arguably the worst holiday of their lives...

One couple didn't have much money for their honeymoon and wanted to avoid any embarrassing fuss, so they booked an ordinary holiday in a small Spanish hotel. On arrival in their room they began to unpack—and have a cuddle as they did so. 'Then I opened the wardrobe door and all hell broke loose,' recalls the bride. 'A man dressed in a gorilla suit leapt out at me! I didn't stop screaming for about half an hour.' It turned out that the gorilla was part of a 'Candid Camera'-style TV programme. 'We felt better once we knew what was going on,' said the bride, 'but after that I had to check the wardrobe and the bathroom before we could even kiss each other...'

Atmosphere and Service

Don't assume that a 'grand' hotel is synonymous with rude, condescending staff. Though something of a cliché, the snooty receptionist and surly waiter unfortunately do still exist. On your honeymoon you want to feel totally at ease, especially if you are splashing out on an expensive room, so pay heed to personal recommendations.

As a matter of course you should expect a turn-down service at night (there's nothing more depressing than an unmade hotel bed), not being disturbed by the maids before 9.30am, a daily supply of fresh, clean towels, and fresh flowers regularly replaced for the duration of your stay. Most of the hotels listed in the following chapters will perform all these services and more. The Mandarin Oriental in San Francisco provide stationery with your name embossed in gold and many UK Relais & Châteaux hotels leave a miniature bottle of scent for female guests; the Amandari in Bali place exquisite gifts by the bed each evening.

A Warm Welcome

There are all-inclusive resorts, particularly in Fiji and the Caribbean, that only accept couples and particularly welcome honeymooners. Hedonism 11, Sandals, and Couples (logo: humping lions) go the whole honeymoon hog, with mirrors on the ceiling, king-size beds, double hammocks—even free weddings.

Opt for a Caribbean cruise and chances are you will be in like-minded company. Couples' names are announced over the tannoy system, there are regular get-togethers with other honeymooners and lots of perks in the drinks department.

Character and Style

And if you can't afford sheer luxury, don't despair. In the following chapters, our '**Hotels Nearby**' listings cover many affordable 3-star hotels and bed-and-breakfasts, all of which have a welcoming atmosphere, discreet service, a pretty setting and comfortable, attractively decorated bedrooms.

There are also state-run *pousadas* in **Spain** and *paradors* in **Portugal** that are full of character. Deceptively simple, these small hotels or inns are often housed in former palaces, stately homes or monasteries. They offer better-than-average food and furnishings and are usually located in beautiful, off-the-beaten-track locations. Though they can be marvellously romantic retreats, you should nevertheless check that your chosen *parador* has double beds. National tourist offices will have details.

In **America** and **Australia** 'boutique' hotels are the equivalent of British townhouse hotels. They are often small, stylish bed-and-breakfast establishments of great individuality; rooms are frequently embellished with antiques and *objets d'art*, and a stay in one of these costs much less than the rates charged by hotel chains.

In the **Caribbean**, you can find gingerbread-style inns, often former plantation homes, and cheaper small guest houses (usually run by an ample matriarch), both of which offer charming personal service and an insight into Caribbean culture.

Crazy Extravagances

These include sunken baths, grand old four-posters, double hammocks, your own plunge pool, a private butler, a 'themed' room. In the Bahamas' Crystal Palace Hotel on Cable Beach, for example, a honeymoon suite takes up a whole floor and includes a robot servant and themed light shows of a tropical storm. On a more modest level, the bathrooms at Cap Juluca on Anguilla have won awards for their double-width marble baths, complete with leather headrests. And the amusingly gothic Huntsham Court hotel in Devon has a wonderful honeymoon room named after the composer Beethoven, with a piano, a huge double bed and an open fire in the bedroom, while the bathroom features two claw-footed Victorian bathtubs.

Adding Up the Cost

Is a suite necessary?

The straightforward answer is: No. Some honeymoon suites are hideously over-the-top, with a price tag to match. If you are into circular beds, satin sheets and cupid wallpaper then go ahead and book, but you will be paying for the décor. In a reliable owner-managed hotel, often the cheapest double room has as much character as the most expensive suite. But if extravagance is an important consideration, always try to find out whether the management has a policy of upgrading honeymooners to a superior room or suite—many do, and it could save you a fortune.

Are packages good value?

Not necessarily. If, however, you like the idea of someone else organising all the romantic little extras, then a package may well suit. Common ingredients include a candlelit dinner for two, chocolates, champagne, flowers, a surprise gift and an outing—a sunset cruise, a limousine tour of the countryside. Bear in mind, however, that many good hotels will provide some of these extras and free transfer to and from the airport as a matter of course.

The best value packages offer incentives like three weeks for the price of two, or interchangeable stays at sister establishments. If you have the time to spare, or like the idea of splitting your time between two hotels, these can represent huge savings. Likewise, all-inclusive packages, particularly at the new breed of upmarket establishments, can provide massive savings on food and activity costs. It is also extremely pleasant not to have to worry about extras, especially on your bar bill.

When should you go?

If you can be flexible with dates, so much the better. Many of the well established honeymoon destinations like the West Indies and East Africa have distinctive seasons that are reflected in the prices quoted by tour operators. But huge savings can be made if you pick a period at the end of the low season. Safaris, for example, can rise to around £600 per person per week after the magic date of 11th December.

The same goes for the Caribbean, where December 15th is the start of high season. Weather changes around this crucial time are never that dramatic—you stand a better chance of a room upgrade at the tail-end of the low season, and of course beaches and organised excursions will be far less crowded.

Will there be extras?

Many hotels still insist on crazy bar prices, which is no fun if you are on a budget, the sun is beating down and you are both hot and thirsty. If in doubt, ask for sample menus before you book—even find out whether there is a good beach bar within walking distance of the hotel; that way, the odd glass of champagne while you peruse the menu won't seem so wickedly extravagant.

If you want your happy news broadcast, you can take advantage of the many special touches extended to honeymooners. Hotel staff will be only too pleased to make a fuss of you, most hotel managers will lay on a bottle of champagne to welcome you, and some may even upgrade you to a larger room or suite.

Adding Up the Cost

What will it cost?

Beware the bargain-sounding package. The tour operator may well be quoting a 'room only' or 'bed-and-breakfast' rate. In some countries, eating out can really stretch the budget, so opt for a minimum of bed-and-breakfast, or a half-board package, which means you can eat either lunch or dinner out. You won't necessarily want a heavy four-course meal every day but, in any case, paying separately for hotel dinners can really push the price up. Some Caribbean resort hotels have 'eat around' schemes, which allow you to dine out at different establishments on the island. These schemes represent an ideal way of getting to know the island, and provide variety to your daily routine.

Hotels are listed in the following four categories; prices are based on a double room per night:

luxury	£300 and above
expensive	£200–300
moderate	£90–190
inexpensive	£40–90

Restaurants are listed in the following three categories, priced per person, based on a two-course meal for two people, with a bottle of table wine and coffee:

expensive	£35 and above
moderate	£15–35
inexpensive	under £15

The Perfect Preparation

In Sickness and in Health

Even minor ill-health on a honeymoon is bound to dull the sparkle. Allow time to check whether any **inoculations** are needed before you travel, and take sensible precautions against the most common problems.

Sunburn can ruin a honeymoon, so pack plenty of high-factor creams. **Mosquitoes** can be a plague on romance so pack repellents, even if you are unsure whether they will be necessary. Take a night-burning coil (Chinese candle) and a mosquito net to infested areas. If you have any doubts about the cleanliness of the **water** or **food**, drink only bottled water, avoid ice, salads, meat (unless well cooked) and street snacks. Pack a simple **first-aid kit**.

For Richer, For Poorer

Don't leave home without your **credit card**. Some hotels insist on them, and ordering room service when you haven't got a credit card can become a real nuisance. Don't travel around with too much **cash** when you go sightseeing and, if in doubt, leave your valuables (sparkling engagement ring, for example) in the hotel's **safety deposit box**.

Good **travel insurance** will give you peace of mind. Make sure the policy gives you full cover for your possessions, and your health as well. If anything gets stolen, you will need a copy of the police report to give to your insurance company back home. Some tour operators provide travel insurance, but check to see whether this cover is adequate for your needs.

Always **label luggage** with your destination address.

You May Now Kiss the Bride

Great expectations can lead to grave disappointments. This is supposedly your 'holiday of a lifetime' but your anticipation can, in itself, work to the detriment of your happiness and well-being while away. It may rain and you will probably argue. You may also feel distinctly tired and consequently very chaste on your honeymoon night, but because tradition dictates otherwise, you might feel guilty. The answer is to go with the flow—treat the honeymoon as just a special holiday—and if things go wrong, rest assured that you will probably end up laughing about your mishaps before the year is out.

Pampering the Bride-to-be

Wedding preparations are very stressful, and it really pays to find a way of unwinding before the ceremony and honeymoon. A smooth transition from high-octane activity to a laid-back honeymoon is often hard to achieve, and some couples complain that the first few days of their trip were 'lost' through sheer exhaustion. If you're flying to your destination, spend the wedding night unwinding at a good hotel near to the airport. And investing in a few days of determined relaxation before the event will undoubtedly be beneficial.

A number of health farms, spas and leisure centres have 'Bridal Top-to-toe' or 'Grooming-the-groom' packages, in which the emphasis is on pampering and relaxation. In the UK and the USA, mother-and-daughter weekends are immensely popular, and hen and stag parties at spas are fast catching on.

Health farms have progressed way beyond those early days when luxury consisted of two lettuce leaves, and water therapy meant alternating between a scalding hot shower and a icy cold dip. Today good healthy food such as prawns, salmon, salads and lean meats, and the odd glass of champagne as well as soothing massage, warm jacuzzis and soporific facials are much more the standard fare.

Crystal Premier Britain, ✆ (0181) 390 8513, arranges affordable long-weekend packages to some of the top UK health spas listed below.

Healthy Venues, ✆ (01203) 690300, can give you information on stag and hen parties, reservations and unbiased advice on all UK health farms.

Spa Finders, ✆ (212) 924 6800, will make bookings at US health spas.

UK Spa Trek

Hoar Cross Hall

Hoar Cross Hall Health Spa, Hoar Cross, Near Yoxall, Staffordshire DE13 8QS, ✆ (01283) 75671. Some discounts for hen and stag parties (depending on numbers) are available through Crystal Premier Britain, ✆ (0181) 390 8513.

At Hoar Cross Hall, a Victorian Tudor-style mansion set in the Staffordshire countryside, 2–7-night stays include a range of treatments for both bride and groom, plus unlimited use of the hydrotherapy pool and whirlpool spa, all heat treatments (sauna, steam room), outdoor badminton, croquet, tennis, boules, 9-hole golf, trim trail, archery classes and bicycles, as well as exercise classes, breakfast, lunch and dinner.

More esoteric treatments that concentrate on stress management range from flotation and aromatherapy to yoga and shiatsu. There are top-to-toe days and make-up lessons. Rooms in the mansion are particularly appealing, with large old-fashioned bedrooms overlooking the formal gardens—there are even rooms with four-poster water-beds.

Henlow Grange

Henlow Grange Health Farm, Henlow, Bedfordshire SG16 6DB, ✆ (01462) 811111.

This red-brick Georgian mansion with its pretty riverside setting is a comfortable place to unwind before the stresses of a wedding. The best bedrooms are in the main house, overlooking the river. There is a small but well-equipped gym, a spectacular new 25-metre swimming pool, as well as facilities for tennis, horse riding, squash, golf and badminton. Exercise classes are gentle, and speciality treatments range from wax baths to Swedish and Thai massage. Most guests are mothers and daughters enjoying time away from the wedding preparations. They opt for top-to-toe days which incorporate plenty of beauty treatments, and long weekend breaks.

The Ideal Hotel

One bride decided that hers was going to be the perfect wedding—and that she was going to be in perfect shape for it. She and her bridesmaid booked themselves into a health farm the week before the wedding for 5 days of pampering.

Between their massages and facials, the women took the opportunity to tone up with workout classes. All went well until, on their last afternoon, the bridesmaid pulled a knee ligament while exercising on one of the weight machines in the gym. Next morning, struggling with both sets of bags down the steps to the car, the bride slipped and broke her ankle. The bride's plans hadn't included the pair of them hobbling down the aisle on crutches...

Champneys

Champneys, Wigginton, Tring, Hertfordshire HP23 6HY, ✆ (01442) 873155.

One of Britain's most established health farms, set in parkland above the vale of Aylesbury, Champneys seems more like a luxury hotel than a spa. The accommodation, even in the modern wing, is of a very high standard and rooms in the main house include sumptuous, tastefully decorated four-poster suites as well as drawing rooms, a study and a billiards room furnished with antiques and 'country house hotel' chintz. Outdoor sporting activities are mountain biking, jogging, tennis, volleyball and nature walks; indoor activities include exercise and relaxation classes—from juggling to Tai Chi Chuan, advice on stress reduction, a Well Woman programme, yoga and first-rate beauty treatments. The Champneys' Facial Treatments for Men incorporate a relaxing massage to the neck and shoulders. Food is healthy and filling, though there is a calorie-controlled menu for those wishing to lose weight before the wedding and honeymoon. Special breaks include reasonably priced men's and women's day programmes, consisting of heat treatment, a session on a sun bed, salt glow treatment and fitness assessments for the groom, and body massage, facial, shampoo, manicure and pedicure for the bride.

US Spa Trek

The range of health spas in the States is enormous. And some of these centres concentrate as much on the well-being of the mind as the body, and offer programmes to benefit all aspects of future wedded bliss.

Tantric Sex Workshop

Source School of Tantra Yoga, PO Box 69, Paia, Maui, HI 96779, ℂ (808) 572 8364.

At the Tantric Sex Workshop in Hawaii, for example, participants are promised new levels of pleasure by studying the 'sacred art of sexual tantra'. Essentially, these couples-only week-long workshops focus on heightening sexual energy through hatha yoga, breathing and energy exercises and practical homework. With its languorous Pacific Ocean setting, this retreat is guaranteed to thaw the most nervous of honeymooners or indeed the chilliest of couples.

Turtle Island Project

The Turtle Island Project, PO Box 41703, Mesa, AZ 85274-1703, ℂ (602) 345 6112.

Brides-to-be and brides' mothers will benefit from a women-only weekend retreat in Arizona. The Turtle Island Project aims to help women discover the 'essence of dynamic feminine power'. The course uses sacred native American rituals and traditions to help participants unwind and get in touch with their inner being.

Ojo Caliente

Ojo Caliente Mineral Springs, PO Box 68, Ojo Caliente, NM 87549, ℂ (800) 222 9162.

For couples wishing to start married life de-toxed, refreshed and completely relaxed, a mineral cleansing weekend in New Mexico could prove hot stuff. Participants soak in natural medicinal springs which bubble up from deep volcanic fissures. Treatments including mud baths and sweat wraps help rid the body of toxins; the food is healthy and the atmosphere pleasingly peaceful.

Doral Saturnia International Spa

Doral Saturnia International Spa, 8755 NW 36th Street, Miami, Florida, ℂ (305) 593 6030.

More orthodox spa programmes that concentrate on pampering and relaxation are available throughout the States, and offer clients as much comfort as a first-class hotel. The Doral Saturnia Spa in Miami is a spectacular example of this genre. Extremely popular with mother-and-daughter teams, the spa is modelled on a traditional Italian villa, with frescoed restaurants, coral-pink jacuzzis, elegant arcading and luxurious suites. Treatments here concentrate on the therapeutic use of mud and thermal water, with an invigorating open-air hydro-massage cascade (like a vigorous car wash), mud wraps, salt rubs and fango facials. Yoga and gentle walking are encouraged more than aerobics, and gourmet low-fat meals of poached lobster and steamed sole are accompanied by a welcome glass or two of Chardonnay.

Honeymoon Hot-spots

The following chapters give specific suggestions for a perfect honeymoon, centred around particular hotels or hotel complexes in some of the world's most romantic summer locations. Detailed descriptions of the hotels' facilities are followed by sightseeing suggestions, alternative accommodation and dining choices and a checklist with all the practical information you need.

Destination Finder

Most locations that have evolved into popular honeymoon choices over recent years have done so with good reason, since they combine a welcoming atmosphere and comfortable hotels with strong activity programmes, generally reliable weather, sightseeing opportunities and romantic surroundings.

beaches

The Caribbean, the Seychelles, Bali, Mauritius, the Maldives, Fiji, Tahiti, Thailand, Goa, Sri Lanka, Italy and Spain.

peace and quiet

The Seychelles, Fiji, Tahiti, Mozambique, Malaysia, Sri Lanka, Zanzibar and Mexico; the Greek islands of Chios, Leros, Lemnos, Paxos, Amorgos and Sifnos; Brittany, Normandy, Ireland, Devon and Cornwall (off season).

interesting islands

The Seychelles (watersports and island-hopping), the Florida Keys (sports, watersports, island-hopping, people watching, shopping), Bora-Bora (watersports, hiking), Fiji (watersports, riding, hiking), Sicily (culture, sports, food, shopping), the Azores (island-hopping, walking, culture), some Greek Islands (island-hopping, culture, watersports), the Bahamas (watersports), the Caribbean (sports, watersports, island-hopping), Zanzibar (culture), Bali (culture, hiking) and Sri Lanka (culture).

outdoor adventure

Alaska, Argentina, Namibia, Borneo, Kenya, China, Australia, the Galapagos islands, India, Venezuela, Mexico, South Africa, Uzbekistan, Vietnam, New England, Brazil and Costa Rica.

city sophistication

Paris, Nice, Florence, Venice, Seville, Madrid, Sydney, Prague, San Francisco, Marrakesh and St Petersburg.

Pura Besakih

Bali

Four Seasons Resort
Jimbaran, Denpasar 80361, Bali
✆ (62 361) 71288
✉ (62 361) 71280
expensive

Amandari
Kedewatan, Ubud, Bali
✆ (62 361) 95333
✉ (62 361) 95335
expensive–moderate

Bali: Jimbaran Bay

Bali is rapidly becoming a favourite destination for honeymooners, being fashionably far-flung for Europeans and a startlingly beautiful island, quirky of culture, exotic and friendly. Peace and privacy are the main attractions for some visitors, including Princess Diana, who when newly separated and world-weary escaped to the secluded and discreet resort of Nusa Dua.

The south, however, is fast developing into a popular tourist haunt. Here, shores of dazzling white sand sheltered by swaying palms, giving way to pounding surf rolling in from India, have helped turn the coast into a thriving, in parts increasingly tinselly, resort colony.

As an alternative to using the southern beaches as a base for your entire honeymoon, split the time between a stay in the hillside village of Ubud (see pp.23–28) and a period at one of the quieter beach hotels, exploring the unspoilt countryside as well as the coast. The island's tiny size—just 90 miles long and 50 miles wide—makes it possible to visit almost every spot on Bali within a day's drive.

Four Seasons Resort

The Four Seasons Resort is a relative newcomer to the island's handful of luxury hotels. Located on Jimbaran Bay, on the Nusa Dua peninsula, it is just 20 minutes' drive from the airport. The place has tremendous visual appeal, with traditional-style thatched buildings terraced into the hillside.

Private Comfort

The Four Seasons' staff are gentle, efficient and charming. Accommodation is in spacious detached **villas** dotted throughout the flower-filled gardens in little village clusters, rising in tiers from the sea. Each villa has 3 pavilions: an outdoor dining-and-resting pavilion, a sleeping pavilion and a bathing pavilion. The views from each of these are magnificent, stretching over the rocky foreshore to Jimbaran Bay and out over Mount Agung, Bali's most sacred mountain.

The **dining-and-resting pavilion** is furnished with a comfortable sofa, a ceiling fan, a table for romantic private meals and an altar in the corner where staff, following Balinese tradition, leave early-morning offerings of fresh fruit and flowers.

Between the two main pavilions is a 12-metre private **plunge pool** and a **sundeck**, sheltered by headily scented frangipani and vivid-hued bougainvillaea, and embellished with ornamental carved animals, water spouting from their mouths in a cool and soothing stream.

In the sleeping pavilion, **beds** are enormous and supremely comfortable, and crowned in a frothy veil of mosquito netting, though air-conditioning effectively keeps biting insects at bay. The high-walled **bathing pavilion**, filled with sweet-smelling jungly plants and flowers, allows for refreshing showers in the open air. Inside, a luxurious marble bathroom has as its centrepiece a big, solid, free-standing oval tub. Jasmine-scented bubble bath, oversized fluffy towels and your own choice of music from the resort's library, create a truly sensual environment.

Public Relaxation

The grounds of the Four Seasons are a marvellous jungle, lovingly cared for by 90 gardeners, with more than 200 different species of plants bursting from colourful beds among Balinese wood carvings and statues. There is a **gym, tennis courts**, a wide variety of watersports and a **spa**. Massages are as much a hedonistic as a therapeutic experience, and include the use of traditional herbal potions. Guests will find themselves covered in a marinade of turmeric, ground nuts and saffron (great for exfoliating the skin), before an enriching layer of cool yoghurt is smoothed over their bodies. The session ends with a soothing warm bath full of rose petals, and a glass of jamu tea to restore vitality.

Eating In

The cuisine consists, for the most part, of the hot and spicy dishes that make up a truly authentic *rijsttafel*. Simpler food, including generous salads, local fish and shellfish and grilled meats, artistically arranged, is also available.

What to See and Do

Jimbaran is a relatively quiet beach situated in the Badung Regency, a narrow isthmus shaped like an exclamation mark that lies in the south, with Bukit, the dot-shaped peninsula, at its apex. Nearby resorts such as **Kuta** tend to be hot, dusty, noisy and fun-loving, which is great if you want fast food, music, cheap massage, street vendors and crowds, but is not ideal for honeymooners in search of peace and privacy. Kuta's beach, however, is most impressive: a vast arc of palm-fringed white sand, with surf rolling continuously and dramatically along the shore. This is not an ideal beach for weak swimmers, but it can be recommended for its dramatic sunsets—everyone gravitates here before dusk to watch the sky change from blood-red to dull gold and silver. After sunset, the

club scene thrives in Kuta. There are open-air beach-front discos and lively bars, many of which keep pounding out the music until almost sunrise.

Nusa Dua on the southeast coast of the Bukit peninsula has some of the best beaches, with long stretches of white sand, shady palm trees and varied watersports. But this area is also characterized by back-to-back international hotels. For more secluded, unspoilt beaches, it is better to head to the east coast, towards the villages of **Manggis** and **Karangesam**, about 50 miles from Jimbaran. Almost the entire coastal stretch here remains undeveloped, except for the area around the celebrated **Amankila Resort Hotel**, with its spectacular 3-tiered, terraced swimming pool. In Sanskrit, Amankila means 'peaceful mountain'. Here, dusty roads skirt the sharp green contours of hills covered with a web of ancient terraces and eventually lead to unspoilt villages where traditional **weaving workshops** turn out hand-dyed *ikat*. Nearby, in Ujung and Tirta Gangga, there are **royal water baths**, built in the forties and offering the coolest, freshest water on the island.

Sanur, directly across the isthmus from Kuta and Legian beaches but still within easy reach of the hills, is a less touristy, more individual resort with a slightly raffish Riviera atmosphere. Village life still thrives, and locals regularly stage **Moon Rising ceremonies** during which everyone gathers to watch the full moon rising over the sea. There are small **boutiques** selling colourful Balinese clothes and crafts, and **restaurants** serving good cheap spicy snacks, running the length of the Jl. Tanjung Sari, the main road through the resort. The local daily **market**, with its stalls selling fruit, vegetables, clothes and spices, also offers a refreshing slice of real Balinese life.

In the east of the island, a newish **corniche** road traces the curve of the coast, past pretty fishing villages and sandy bays, providing spectacular sightseeing. If you drive south down this road you reach **Candi Dasa**, where there is a small, picturesque, relatively peaceful beach with cheap restaurants serving good-quality food. Behind the lagoon that lies at the eastern end of the beach is a traditional Balinese **temple** dedicated to the goddess Hariti.

Eating Out

The Tandjung Sari, on Jl. Tanjung Sari, PO Box 25, Denpasar 80001, © (62 361) 88441 (*moderate*). This small family hotel serves real Indonesian food in a courtyard setting. The saté and *rijsttafel* are particularly good.

Hotels Nearby

Amankila, Manggis, Bali, © (62 366) 21993.

Bali: Ubud

Ubud Bali woodcarver

Bali is famous for its tropical palm-fringed beaches, but it is the island's interior that offers a slice of authentic Indonesian life. For couples who like to sightsee as well as sunbathe, the small hill town of Ubud provides a convenient and culturally interesting base. Ubud has attracted artists, dancers and craftsmen over many years, and consequently is now rich in museums and galleries, markets and crafts shops. The town is within an hour's drive of the coastal resorts, in the fertile, cooler foothills of the south, amid beautiful rice terraces. Walking, hiking and mountain-biking to neighbouring villages are all possible.

Amandari

The Amandari is a truly luxurious hotel situated next to the village of Kedewatan, just 5 minutes' drive northwest of Ubud's centre. Designed in the fashion of a walled Balinese village, it looks down some 250 feet into the dramatic Ayung river gorge. Fanning out in the distance are the intensely green, serpentine contours of the rice terraces.

Guests are met from the airport in colourful jeeps. Thoughtful touches, which are a characteristic of the Amandari's high standards of service, include cooling wet face towels for the journey—refreshing after a long flight. Guests receive a constant supply of these towels as well as fresh orchids in their rooms each day.

Private Comfort

There are 29 suites divided into 3 types—the single-level **terrace suite** with private garden area; the **duplex suite**, with spacious sitting room opening on to a private garden and spiral staircase leading to the upstairs bedroom; and the **pool duplex suite** with its own swimming pool.

All the suites are well designed and private. The duplex suites are, however, very appealing. You feel like a house guest in a spacious annexe, without suffering the need to socialize or the burden of having to please your host. Cool marble floors and elegant timber interiors come furnished with modern Balinese-style fittings: comfortable cream day-beds stacked with cushions, hand-carved, canopied double beds, decorative wall hangings, rattan armchairs and wicker baskets. All have air-conditioning, bamboo- and palm-thatched roofs, and stunning sunken marble **outdoor tubs**, enclosed by a high wall and surrounded by exotic flora and fauna. Fragrant frangipani flowers float across the water's surface; delicious-smelling coconut soaps and unguents, cool cotton robes and stylish slippers are provided for each guest. At dusk, while guests drink cocktails and listen to the soft chimes of a gamelan orchestra, the staff busily tidy and embellish each suite. A **gift**, changing every day, is left on a pillow—not the ubiquitous luxury chocolate found in European hotels, but an orchid bloom perhaps, or a delicious Indonesian sweetmeat nestling at the bottom of a miniature bamboo basket or an exquisite toy grasshopper woven from delicately split palm fronds, or an unusual local fruit, peeled to resemble a rosebud.

Public Relaxation

The Amandari's other facilities include a large **swimming pool** with contours that echo those of the neighbouring rice terraces, a floodlit **tennis court**, an antique **gallery** selling Indonesian arts and crafts, a well-stocked **library** and a **bar**. The hotel will arrange bicycling, walking, rafting and shopping trips to Ubud and nearby towns and villages.

Eating In

The Amandari has a spacious verandah restaurant overlooking the gardens and the swimming pool. The cuisine served here ranges from **European** to piquant **Indonesian**, with specialities including tasty noodles and juicy fish saté.

What to See and Do

A good starting point for information on the area is the Bina Wisata **tourist office** on a road called Jalan Ubud at the centre of town (*open daily except Sun*). The staff will help with itineraries, transport and maps, and will advise on local cultural events.

There has always been a thriving local community of sculptors, woodcarvers and artists, who originally worked for Ubud's royal family and decorated nearby temples. Today, the town has a more international artistic flavour, with many Western artists settling and exhibiting here. The **Museum Puri Lukisan** (*open daily 8–4pm*) is situated near the centre in beautiful tropical gardens, and shows a varied and historical range of Balinese art. The **Neka Gallery** (*open daily, 8.30–5pm*), 2km north of the centre near the village of Campuan, is a good place to buy high quality Balinese art. It also has temporary and permanent exhibits of Balinese and Western art.

There are lots of interesting **shops** along Monkey Forest Road, selling woodcarvings and masks. Batik-printed clothes, fabrics, tablecloths and woven bedcovers made in Ubud are also good affordable souvenirs. The **market** takes place along the main street every third day and is well worth visiting. Pungent spices and herbs, dirt-cheap sandals and clothes, as well as livestock (especially pigs) and dried fish are sold here.

Some of the best **gamelan orchestras and dancers** come from Ubud, and regular performances, temple ceremonies and dance-dramas are staged both in and near the town. The Bina Wisata office will have details of what is on each day and how to get there.

One of Bali's most ancient temples is located near Campuan Bridge. Almost hidden by greenery, **Pura Gunung Labah** is thought to have been founded in the 8th century by the Javanese Shivaite priest, Danghyang Markandeya. It is a wonderful cool refuge on hot days, and during festivals the whole area around the bridge is flooded with colour and crowds.

A leisurely walk through the **Monkey Forest**, off Monkey Forest Road, brings you into contact with its noisy but charming-looking inhabitants. However, these small grey monkeys can be vicious if provoked, so keep your distance and don't feed them. The forest itself is wonderfully lush and peaceful; there is a temple on its west side, the **Pura Dalem**, which is theatrically hidden by creepers.

Hiking through Ubud is immensely rewarding. The area to the west of town, covering Campuan, Penestanan, Sayan and Kedewatan, is fairly easy going, and offers a walk of no more than 5 miles. You pass picturesque gorges, the Pura Gunung Labah (temple), and the villages of Penestanan and Sayan which run alongside rice terraces. The fast-flowing Ayung river is refreshing to **bathe** in on a baking hot day.

A 3-mile hike north of Ubud leads to the villages of Petulu and Junjungan. Petulu is named after a large flock of herons which nest here. Try to catch them flying in formation—an unforgettable sight. Junjungan is remarkably unspoilt and surrounded by a verdant landscape of bamboo, rocks, grass and rivers which is an ideal setting for picnics.

Eating Out

Murni's Warung, down by the Campuan Bridge (*inexpensive*), is an established restaurant with an extensive Western and Balinese menu. Try their frozen banana cheesecake.

Ubud Restaurant, Monkey Forest Road (*inexpensive*), serves Balinese food that has been adapted to Western palates. Excellent pork saté with coconut is offered.

Hotels Nearby

★★★★★**Kupu Kupu Barong**, in Kedewatan. Jl. Kecubung 72, Denpasar, Bali, © (62 361) 23172. Stunningly positioned on the edge of the Ayung River valley, this hotel has traditionally designed individual houses with private jacuzzi pools.

Checklist

when to go

Bali is just over 8° south of the Equator. Coastal breezes help to temper the tropical heat and Ubud, in the mountainous interior, is generally much cooler than Jimbaran Bay on the coast. Temperatures average around 26°C in the shade. Bali is at its most brilliant from **April until**

September, during the dry season, though it may still rain in these months. In the wet season, from October to March, it can rain continuously, the roads often turn to mud, and the heat tends to be quite oppressively muggy.

getting there

By air: Garuda Indonesia flies direct from London and from Los Angeles to Bali's only airport, Ngurah Rai, to the south of Denpasar. Other carriers from the UK include KLM (changing at Amsterdam), and Swissair and Qantas (changing at Jakarta).

Transfers to and from the airport are available to guests of the Four Seasons Resort and the Amandari.

tour operators

From the UK, packages for both Bali destinations are available through **Abercrombie & Kent Ltd**, Sloane Square House, Holbein Place, London SW1W 8NS, ✆ (0171) 730 9600, and **Airwaves**, 10 Bective Place, London SW15 2PZ, ✆ (0181) 875 1188.

From the US, packages are available through **Abercrombie & Kent International Inc.**, 1420 Kensington Road, Oak Brook, Illinois 60521, ✆ (312) 954 1944.

booking direct

Reservations for the Regent can be made from the UK, freefone ✆ (0800) 526 648 and from the USA, toll-free ✆ (800) 332 3442.

entry formalities

UK, US and Canadian citizens need full passports.

health

Immunization against cholera, typhoid, polio, hepatitis A, and antimalarial tablets are recommended. Sterilize drinking water.

getting around

Car hire is recommended and is comparatively cheap. A jeep is best for tackling the more remote regions. There are numerous agencies in Denpasar and Sanur. **Bicycle** and **car**

hire can be arranged through the Amandari.

In Ubud, there is no public transport system and the town is easy and pleasant to walk around, laid out on a grid-like sytem evolving from the two main roads, the Jl. Raya from Denpasar and Monkey Forest Road.

getting by

The main languages are **Bahasa Indonesia** and **Bahasa Bali** but **English** is widely spoken. The Indonesian currency is the **rupiah**. **US dollars** and major credit cards are accepted at resort hotels and restaurants.

getting married

Marriages can be performed here.

England: Cumbria

Sharrow Bay Country House Hotel
Lake Ullswater, Penrith, Cumbria CA10 2LZ
✆ (017684) 86301
✉ (017684) 86349
moderate–expensive

The poet Wordsworth called Lakeland 'the loveliest spot that man hath ever found', and few would disagree with him today. In fact ever since the late 18th century, when Wordsworth and his fellow Romantic poets immortalised the region in vivid verse, Lakeland has remained popular with visitors.

Such popularity inevitably brings speedboats, waterskis and crowds in good weather but Ullswater has successfully managed to avoid most of the pitfalls of tourism. Here, honeymooners can be guaranteed a tremendously peaceful retreat. Birds, ducks and sheep are often the only company in this unspoilt and romantic landscape; the comparatively gentle hills offer walks suitable even for inexperienced hikers, and the spectacular lake itself is big enough for crowd-free sailing and canoeing.

Sharrow Bay Country House Hotel

This hotel has an idyllic setting at the water's edge on the extreme eastern side of the lake; the staff positively pride themselves on their ability to cosset and comfort. Guests are greeted with a couple of glasses of sherry and a welcome card in their bedrooms, and poems are placed on pillows last thing at night. Written by one of Sharrow Bay's charming owners, they bid you to be happy and relaxed, to enjoy the peaceful atmosphere and awake refreshed, full of good thoughts for the day.

The hotel was built in 1840, and remained a private home until 1949. It has an unusual architectural style, with low-angled roof-ridges and wide eaves on the lakeside frontage, giving it the feel of a Swiss chalet or a holiday villa set on the shores of Italy's Lake Como. Inside is a maze of smallish rooms crammed with ornaments, clocks, amateur Victorian watercolours and vases of flowers. There are two comfortable lounges housing an oddball collection of sofas, armchairs and settles, a conservatory where guests can take their coffee after dinner, as well as a couple of handsome and unusual dining rooms. The service throughout the hotel is faultless. Waiters appear genuinely concerned if your appetite fails to meet the demands of the menu, and receptionists are particularly helpful in suggesting interesting itineraries for outings.

Private Comfort

Upstairs, the 12 **bedrooms** vary in size, some even boasting their own private **balcony**, but none is particularly large. In keeping with the credo of the hotel, the emphasis is on cosiness, with chintzy furniture and furnishings evoking the atmosphere of a post-war country cottage: a pile of books on a small carved wooden table; knick-knacks arranged at random on chests, table tops and mantelpieces; a pretty tin

England: Cumbria

filled with home-made shortbread, set beside a porcelain dish filled to the brim with pastel-coloured sugared almonds.

Silver is one of the larger bedrooms, and takes its name from the silver flock wallpaper and painted furniture in the bedroom. Both this and the pretty **bathroom** overlook the lake. A couple of comfy sofas are thoughtfully placed either side of the window frame so that you can enjoy the magnificent view. A handful of small yachts bob on the water's surface; two boys sit fishing on a wooden jetty. The sun glints off the water in a lake so clear that you can see the pebbles at the bottom, even from these first-floor rooms.

Public Relaxation

Guests can take pre-dinner drinks either outside on the **terrace**, where the waves of Ullswater lap at the wall of soft grey stone or in one of the **lounges**. Restraint is advisable with the delicious canapés, including hot cheese *beignets* and miniature pizzas, since the cooking at Sharrow Bay is on the rich side.

The **lakeside dining-room**, panelled in dark wood and with tiled insets, has yet more glorious views of the lake—and it is sheer magic to watch the changing light on water as the evening meal progresses. Across from the kitchen, the other **dining-room** is handsome and comfortable. Converted from a billiard room, it has an unusual high wooden ceiling, fine antiques and tapestry chairs.

Not all guests stay in the main hotel. There is an Edwardian lodge with bedrooms and suites, a garden cottage by the shore, and a charming 17th-century Quaker cottage in the neighbouring village of Tirril; and Bank House, just a mile and a quarter from the hotel. This former Elizabethan farmhouse has a magnificent beamed breakfast room converted from a barn, with a grand stone fireplace originally from Warwick Castle. Bank House offers greater seclusion, since it lies at the end of the eastern 'finger' of Ullswater, and very few tourists travel this far along the single-track road. In the comfortable living room, copies of Wainwright's walking guides to the fells stand alongside recent editions of *Vogue* and helpful pamphlets on what to see and do in Ullswater. Guests can take their drinks here by the fire, or outside in fine weather, before driving to the main hotel for dinner.

Eating In

British produce, albeit cooked in a somewhat dated French manner, is Sharrow Bay's forte. Heavy starters such as a ravioli of lobster *mousseline* precede main courses of duckling and herb-crusted lamb, with a fish and a sorbet course in between. Some of the simpler dishes, such as the sautéed scallops, are superb. Rather eccentrically, the waitress 'talks you through' the puddings displayed on a table by the restaurant entrance before you even reach your table. There is a fixed, 5-course menu, which, at £41.50, is not cheap, though dinner is included in the room rate, and most guests work up a nightly appetite with long hikes in the hills or boat trpis during the day. Breakfasts are equally belt-busting (an ideal start for a day on the fells) as are Sharrow Bay's picnic baskets, with delicious sandwiches, home-made biscuits, fruit and cheese.

What to See and Do

Sharrow Bay is a good starting point for tours of the lakes—a haven for hikers, cyclists, anglers and yachting fanatics. There are **walks** to suit everybody. Low-level routes include hikes around the lake itself, for example from Howtown to Glenridding (7 miles). From Howtown, walk back on the footpath along the shore and through the woods. The path is easy to find and takes in the magnificent scenery of Ullswater and the hills, with Helvellyn rising above the wooded foothills. More ambitious hill-walking is available at Helvellyn, St Sunday Crag and Fairfield, off the A592. The hotel will provide guests with detailed itineraries. Before you begin any walk, do make sure you take the correct safety precautions, take into account the weather conditions and wear suitable clothing and footwear.

MY *Raven* and MY *Lady of the Lake* are two pretty 19th-century steamers, now converted to **oil-cruising** on Ullswater. In full season, there are 3 scheduled services daily between Glenridding, Howtown and Pooley Bridge. There are also 5 shorter, 1-hour cruises from Glenridding, calling at Howtown, and an extra evening cruise, departing Glenridding at 5.45pm during July and August. A landing stage for these cruises is at the foot of Bank House. For more information, call Ullswater Navigation and Transit Company, ✆ (017684) 82229.

Howtown Outdoor, ✆ (017684) 86508, offer organised day activities in the Ullswater region (*from £35 per day*), including abseiling, canoeing, fell walking, gorge walking, mountaineering, mountain guiding, orienteering, rock scrambling, and sailing on the lakes.

David Fallowfield Chauffeur Drive Service, ✆ (01768) 866656, can arrange individual day-long itineraries for **exploring** the region. Day trips cover a Wordsworth or Beatrix Potter Lakeland Tour (*both approx 6 hours*), the Yorkshire Dales, John Peel Country and the West Coast of Cumbria.

There are some fascinating **historic houses**, all easily accessible from the hotel. Good for wet days is a trip to **Hill Top** near Sawrey, Ambleside, ✆ (015394) 36269 (*open daily, April–Oct; from Ullswater, take A592 to Windermere, then A591, A593 and B5286 to Hawkshead*). This little house belonged to the celebrated children's author, Beatrix Potter. Potter wrote many of her books here, and the 17th-century house contains her furniture and china.

Dove Cottage, ☎ (015394) 35544 (*open daily, mid-Feb–mid-Jan*), is set back from the shores of Grasmere just off the A591, 250 yards south of Grasmere village. This was Wordsworth's home during his most prolific years. It is beautifully preserved and the garden, 'a little nook of mountain ground', is also open, weather permitting. The adjacent **Wordsworth Museum** has manuscripts, paintings and memorabilia relating to the poet, as well as a well-stocked book and gift shop, perfect for snapping up a tome of Romantic poems to accompany a gentle walk through the fells.

Levens Hall and World-Famous Topiary Garden, ☎ (015395) 60321 (*open 2 April–28 Sept, Sun–Thurs*), is situated by Levens Bridge on the A6, 5 miles south of Kendal (exit 36 from the M6). Levens Hall is an Elizabethan house with fine Jacobean furniture, superb panelling, plasterwork and ceilings. The shrubbery, laid out during the reign of Charles II, is certainly worth a visit.

Also good for gardens is **Sizergh Castle**, ☎ (015395) 60070 (*open April–Oct, Sun–Thurs afternoons*), 3½ miles south of Kendal (northwest interchange A590/591). Inside, the oldest part of the castle dates from the 14th century, and there is a fine collection of Elizabethan furniture, paintings and carvings.

Eating Out

Leeming House Restaurant, Watermillock, Ullswater, nr Penrith, ☎ (017684) 86622 (*moderate*), offers English cooking with French style.

The Old Church Hotel, Wattermillock, Ullswater, nr Penrith, ☎ (017684) 86204 (*moderate*), specializes in British cooking with an emphasis on local ingredients.

Hotels Nearby

*****Michael's Nook**, Grasmere, Ambleside, Cumbria LA22 9RP, ☎ (015394) 35496 (*expensive–moderate*), is a fine, early Victorian Lakeland house. Dove Cottage is less than a mile away, and Beatrix Potter's home at Sawrey is only a short drive.

*****The Linthwaite House Hotel**, Bowness-on-Windermere, Cumbria, LA23 3JA, ☎ (015394) 88600 (*moderate*). This stylish, affordable Lakeland house with fine views of Windermere.

Connect With

*****Kinnaird**, by Dunkeld (*see* pp.125–130).

Checklist

when to go

May and June are recommended—they are warm, quiet months, and the dazzling azaleas and pale purple rhododendrons are at their loveliest then.

getting there

By air: Birmingham Airport is about 3 hours' drive; Manchester International Airport is 2 hours' drive.

By rail: Penrith Station (7 miles away) is served by frequent Intercity services from major cities such as London, Birmingham, Manchester, Liverpool and Edinburgh.

By road: Sharrow Bay is 7 miles from Penrith. Take exit 40 off the M6, and then the A592 to Pooley Bridge. The hotel is 2 miles from Pooley Bridge; follow the signs for Martindale. Using the motorways, the average journey time from London (295 miles away) and the Southeast is about 5 hours.

booking direct

From the USA, reservations can be made through the **Relais & Châteaux** New York Sales Office, ✆ (212) 8560115.

entry formalities

US and Canadian citizens need full passports.

getting around

Car hire is recommended. Cars can be ordered to await your arrival at any station or at the hotel, ✆ (015394) 88002 for more details. Free local delivery and collection is offered by Cumbria Car Rental, ✆ (015394) 44408.

getting by

The currency is the **pound sterling**. Sharrow Bay does not accept credit cards. Cash and cheques supported by a cheque guarantee card are accepted.

England: Cumbria

England: Burgh Island, Devon

Burgh Island Hotel
Burgh Island, Bigbury-on-Sea, South Devon TQ7 4AY
✆ (01548) 810514
📠 (01548) 810243
moderate

Island retreats are extremely popular with honeymooners, evoking as they do privacy, adventure and romance, sun, sea and sand. But for a dramatic, eccentric and altogether British alternative to the sun-drenched islands of the Caribbean and the Indian Ocean, and one that would combine effortlessly with a touring honeymoon through the English countryside, Burgh Island in England's West Country is absolutely ideal.

Burgh Island is a tiny 26-acre rocky protrusion located off the South Devon coastline, opposite the small seaside village of Bigbury-on-Sea. Twice a day, the water recedes to reveal a passage of golden sand connecting the island to the mainland. At low tide you can simply walk across, but when the waters are high you are transported over in an enormous, ancient sea tractor, an extraordinary machine, with wheels on the ends of stilts and a noisily throbbing engine, that could have been culled from the imagination of Heath Robinson. It is a wonderfully theatrical way to travel, particularly when the weather is rough and the island's distinctive Art Deco hotel is shrouded by a smoky swirling veil of mist.

One romantic groom blindfolded his new wife and, at the dead of night, hired a helicopter to deliver her across the sea passage to Burgh Island. She had no idea where she was, nor whether the hotel was in England, the Channel Islands or France!

Burgh Island Hotel

The Burgh Island hotel is a gem of Art Deco extravagance. Lovingly restored by its owners, Thea and Tony Porter, it has appeared in numerous period films including adaptations of Agatha Christie novels. Indeed, the celebrated crime writer set 2 of her stories on the island: *Evil under the Sun* and *And Then There Were None*.

The island itself has an interesting history. Like St Michael's Mount off Cornwall, it was once a holy island, with a monastery and chapel occupying the site of the present hotel. The first hotel was constructed of timber in 1895 by the island's then owner, a well known music hall singer called George Chirgwin. The building still stands and is used by the hotel staff. After Chirgwin died, the hotel was taken over by the army during the First World War, after which the island passed into the hands of a rich industrialist called Archibald Nettlefold. Among his other interests, Nettlefold owned the Comedy Theatre in London, where Agatha Christie's plays were being staged. Through the author, he became acquainted with members of the jet set, many of whom came to stay on Burgh Island. To accommodate them all, Nettlefold commissioned the architect Matthew Dawson to design a 'great white palace'—the hotel that exists today. As well as Christie, regular guests of the time included Noël Coward, Lord Mountbatten and Edward Prince of Wales, who brought Wallis Simpson to the island in a bid to escape the attentions of the press.

The island's fame spread, and the place acquired the reputation of being rather racy. On summer evenings, big bands would row out to the island's diving platform in the centre of the Mermaid rock pool and play the top tunes of the day, while guests sipped cocktails at the water's edge.

Private Comfort

Each of the 14 **suites** enjoys a magnificent sea view. Most have a sitting room and balcony as well as a bedroom and bathroom, and the **furnishings** are authentically Art Deco, albeit occasionally in rather a tatty condition. Though by no means luxurious, the hotel is charmingly individual throughout.

Public Relaxation

Burgh Island Hotel has changed little over the years. With its candy-coloured walls and curvilinear shapes it resembles a gargantuan ice-cream cake, though once inside you quickly feel as if you have stepped on board an ocean-going liner from the thirties. The ground floor houses the splendid **Palm Court**, with its domed stained-glass 'peacock' ceiling, mirrored twenties **cocktail bar** and lime-coloured Lloyd Loom chairs. Guests assemble here in the evening for dotty-sounding drinks like 'Flappers' Delight', though in warm weather the **outdoor terrace** overlooking the Mermaid rock pool—the hotel's **natural swimming pool**, becomes a venue for pre-dinner cocktails.

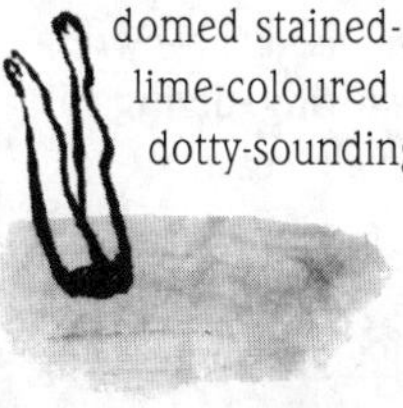

An air of faded grandeur and deep nostalgia pervades the hotel. Guests are asked to wear a jacket and tie or preferably evening dress to dinner, and those who take the plunge into total authenticity with strings of pearls, feather boas and white dinner-jackets score huge plus points with the management.

The hotel has its own **shop**, selling original twenties and thirties memorabilia including old leather suitcases, scarves, hats and costume jewellery. There is a small **gym**, a **sauna** and **sunbed**, a full-sized **snooker table**, a **tennis court** and a **reading room**.

Eating In

The hotel has a magnificent **ballroom**, accessible from the foyer via a wide staircase flanked by pink mirrors and black glass, and this is where dinner is served to a background of contemporary tunes. Since this is an island hotel, dinner is included in the room rate, and the food is extremely reasonable: local fish and shellfish feature prominently in an eclectic and interesting menu.

What to See and Do

Burgh Island is a delight to **walk** around and takes no more than an hour of easy strolling. The island was a notorious haunt for smugglers over the centuries and one in particular, called Tom Crocker, had a secret passage on the island, where he kept his buried treasure. Guests might find it amusing to go searching for Crocker's cave and, when they fail to find it, to content themselves with gazing on Crocker's portrait hanging on the right-hand side of the fireplace in the **Pilchard Inn**—Burgh Island's historic and only pub.

The island is covered with **wild flowers** during spring and summer, and the offshore rock known as '**Little Island**' is home to some rare species of **birds**. Burgh Island is steep and rocky, and the most jagged rocks are found at the western tip where the surf pounds dramatically, whatever the weather. Indeed, many ships have been wrecked on these rocks over the centuries. **Swimming** is safe and enjoyable in the Mermaid pool; during hot weather this lagoon becomes a blissfully sheltered suntrap, used only by residents and hidden by towering rocks. **Windsurfing**, **diving** and **dinghy sailing** are all offered on the island's main beach.

Interesting sites and towns in South Devon are easily accessible from the mainland, on manageable day trips. **Salcombe**, approximately 10 miles from Bigbury following the A381, is the most southerly town in Devon and well known as a sailing centre and holiday resort. There are good beaches, great coastal walks, watersports, a wide range of shops flanking tiny cobbled lanes, and reliable fish restaurants. The fishing port of **Dartmouth** is about 15 miles away from Burgh Island, and can be reached via the A379 coast road. The town centre is rich in historical buildings from the 17th century, the old market place stages a bustling market on Tuesday and Friday and there are pleasure-boat trips either upstream, where much of the British television series *The Onedin Line* was filmed, or along the coast to watch the grey seals.

Buckfast Abbey, Buckfastleigh, Devon, ✆ (01364) 642519 (*open daily, 9–5.30pm*), is about 16 miles from Bigbury (A381 to Totnes, then A384). This Benedictine monastery is famous for its beekeeping, stained glass and tonic wine, has a magnificent Abbey Church, tranquil grounds, a well-stocked souvenir shop and a restaurant.

Eating Out

The Pilchard Inn, Burgh Island (*inexpensive*) is the island's one and only pub/bistro, serving simple hot meals.

Spinnakers Waterside Restaurant & Bar, Fore Street, Salcombe, ✆ (01548) 843408 (*inexpensive*). The speciality here is very fresh grilled fish—choose your own from the display.

Buckland-tout-Saints Hotel, Goveton, Kingsbridge, ✆ (01548) 853055 (*expensive*). This elegant Queen Anne manor house serves award-winning English and French cuisine.

Connect With

Summer Lodge, Dorset (*see* pp.41–46).

One couple booked a beautiful-looking and very pricey hotel on the strength of a brochure. When they got there they found that the sash windows were draughty and rattled at the slightest breeze, the heavily chintzed 'dressing table' concealed a rickety mess of plywood and staples underneath, and, worst of all, the bedsprings were ancient and creaky beneath the crisply ironed sheets and flounced floral pillowcases. The hotel is now in the hands of receivers...

Checklist

when to go

Summer is the best season to visit Burgh Island. Though the location can be extraordinarily romantic in rough winter weather, with the sound of the waves crashing against the rocks and the sense of being a true island castaway, the colder months do limit guests to indoor activities. In contrast, warm summer weather makes swimming a delightful experience in the island's sheltered coves, and South Devon itself offers plenty of interesting locations for day trips.

getting there

By road: Three and a half hours from London. Take the M5 to Exeter/A38 towards Plymouth. Exit at Wrangaton and follow signs for Modbury and Bigbury-on-Sea. At St Ann's Chapel, call the island from the callbox and alert the sea tractor.

By air: Chas Clark Helicopters fly direct to Burgh Island, ✆ 01860 745434.

By rail: Regular services to Plymouth run from London Paddington, the Midlands and the north. Collection and transport to the island can be arranged upon request.

entry formalities

US and Canadian citizens need full passports.

getting by

The currency is the **pound sterling.** Major credit cards are accepted.

England: Dorset

Summer Lodge
Evershot, Dorset DT2 OJR
✆ (01935) 83424
📠 (01935) 83005
moderate–expensive

For lovers of the gentle English countryside so vividly described by Thomas Hardy, Dorset will prove an ideal summer retreat. Though the 19th-century author adopted the name 'Wessex' to describe the home county of his characters—'a partly real, partly dream country'—many of the bustling towns and sleepy villages are recognizable as Dorset, and much of their rural charm has remained unchanged over the years. This is a county of rolling hillsides, dramatic cliffs, sweeping pebble beaches and quiet country lanes; rich, too, in history, legend and local attractions. It enjoys a peaceful unhurried atmosphere, and so is suited to both short breaks and stays of a week or more.

Evershot is accessible via the Dorset town of Yeovil, located right in the heart of the West of England—from where you pass through some wonderful-sounding places like Ryme Intrinseca and Mudford Sock. Sadly, these villages fail to live up to their eccentric and extravagant names, though Evershot itself is gratifyingly unspoilt. Here, Hardy's heroine *Tess of the d'Urbevilles* called at a cottage to ask for breakfast on her way to Beaminster—and sure enough you will find a cottage named 'Tess's Cottage'. Pretty cottages and fine Georgian houses straddle the tiny narrow high street. There is a pub and village shop, and Evershot finally ends at the church, beyond which are miles of rolling fields and woodlands.

Summer Lodge

An attractive, white-painted Georgian dower house, Summer Lodge was originally built by the 2nd Earl of Ilchester. The 17 bedrooms, decorated in a country cottage style, are all generously proportioned, and enjoy pretty views over the gardens and rooftops of Evershot. In 1893, the 6th Earl of Ilchester decided to enlarge the house. He commissioned his friend, the local author and architect Thomas Hardy, to draw up plans for a new drawing room and master bedroom. Honeymooners get upgraded to this or other better rooms whenever possible, and champagne and flowers are provided free of charge. The staff are exceptionally friendly and no request is too much trouble; when you leave, the charmingly eccentric owner–manager, Nigel Corbett, is likely to wave you goodbye and, in the manner of an affectionate uncle, continue waving until you are a speck in the distance. Few extras are added to the bill: morning tea, newspapers, a lavish Dorset cream tea and tennis are all included.

Private Comfort

The **master bedroom** (room 1) is quite the loveliest room in the hotel, and on warm nights in May abundant fronds of wisteria shroud its enormous window, sending in wafts of luxuriously heady scent. This is an incredibly spacious bedroom, so large that even the majestic canopied bed seems lost in such generous surroundings. The centrepiece of this utterly romantic room is an elegant marble fireplace surrounded by comfortable squashy sofas; on cooler evenings a log fire is lit for guests. There is a pretty **bathroom** with decorative blue tiles, giant bottles of herbal foam bath to soothe away wedding-day tensions, and bath towels the size of blankets. Next door a tray is set ready for making tea, with delicate china, homemade shortbread and real milk.

Porcelain cheese dishes decorate the mantelpiece—indeed, the whole hotel is rather eccentrically given over to the celebration of all things cheese-related. Cheese dishes are displayed in all shapes and sizes, from those of dinky doll's-house proportions to elaborately grand examples.

Public Relaxation

Public rooms at Summer Lodge are wonderfully old-fashioned, very Noël Coward in atmosphere, with large sash windows giving views on to the croquet lawn, twenties furniture and floral displays. The **morning room**, with its pile of dog-eared copies of *Country Life* and parish newspapers, is the setting for morning coffee and pre-dinner drinks. There is a snug **library**, commandeered by the hotel's ever-snoozing ginger cat. Outside there are **tennis courts**, well-tended **gardens** and a small, forlorn and freezing open-air **swimming pool**.

Eating In

Food is appetising and extremely skillfully cooked, with an emphasis on all things **British**. Fresh local produce is used where possible, and the cheeseboard served in the dining room includes Cornish Yarg and Dorset Blue Vinney.

What to See and Do

There are many fine and celebrated **stately homes** nearby, both family-run and National-Trust owned, that are open to the public.

On fine days, **Parnham House**, Beaminster, ✆ (01308) 862204 (*open Sun, Weds and Bank Holidays, April–Oct, 10 –5pm*), is worth a visit. This enchanting Tudor manor is now home to John Makepeace, the renowned designer, and his talented team of furniture makers. If your budget doesn't quite run to commissioning a double bed, there is a fine crafts shop for smaller items. The house is also surrounded by appealing gardens.

Hardy's Cottage, Higher Bockhampton, near Dorchester, ✆ (01305) 262366 (*open daily except Thurs, 1 April–31 Oct*), is the author's woodland thatched cottage, where he was born in 1840. It is a good venue for wet days.

Details of established **Thomas Hardy tours** and a new **Hardy trail** are available from the Thomas Hardy Society, PO Box 1438, Dorchester DT1 1YH.

Dorchester itself should not be missed. The setting for Hardy's *The Mayor of Casterbridge*, it has some elegant 18th-century houses, good souvenir shops, and is also home to the **County Museum**, which boasts the most comprehensive collection of Hardyana in the world.

For enthusiastic walkers the **Dorset Coast Path**, which runs from Lyme Regis to Poole Harbour, provides a varied and colourful route, taking in beaches and the famous rock formations at Lulworth Cove and Durdle Door, as well as interesting seaside towns. It is the shortest section of the South West Peninsula Coast Path. The whole walk can be covered in a few days, but shorter day or afternoon treks can be started from any convenient car park, and signposting is clear along the length of the walk. *The Dorset Coastal Path*, produced by the Countryside Commission and published by HMSO, contains sections of the relevant Ordnance Survey maps and a detailed account of the route, and is available from most of the local bookshops.

For a romantically nostalgic tour of the county, **Scenic Vintage Tours**, Whitchurch Canonicorum, Dorset, ✆ (01297) 489116, offer tailor-made itineraries in a classic vintage tourer.

Fishing is good at Lyme Regis, or Chesil Beach, and inland there are well-stocked lakes. The **Tourist Information Centre** in Dorchester, located in Acland Road, ✆ (01305) 267992, will hold details of these, as well as the region's numerous **riding centres** and **stables, golf courses** and **hang-gliding centres**. For details of **hot-air ballooning,** contact Hot Air Balloon Flights, 3 Downes Street, Bridport, Dorset, ✆ (01308) 45806.

Nigel Corbett at Summer Lodge is the fount of all local knowledge, and will arm you with maps, suggested routes, and delicious champagne picnics. The drive to **Lyme Regis**, 20 miles from the hotel on the B3163/4 and B3165, takes you through the rolling green Dorset countryside, and offers spectacular panoramas of the landscape as well as the sea in the far distance. The route is punctuated by prosperous little Georgian towns, including handsome Beaminster, with its 200 listed buildings, tiny Broadwindsor and the sheer white chalk cliffs and cosy narrow streets of Lyme itself.

Eating Out

The Riverside Restaurant, West Bay, nr Bridport, Dorset, ✆ (01308) 422011 (*moderate–inexpensive*), is a casual, relaxed, fun restaurant, where lobsters and local rockers meet. Simple grilled plaice and chips, sole and cod, as well as thick fish soup, are the best choices.

Polly Victoria, 15 Marine Parade, Lyme Regis, ✆ (01297) 442886 (*inexpensive*), is a tiny, unpretentious restaurant, good for fish lunches and suppers. Meat and vegetarian dishes are also available.

Hotels Nearby

★★★Alexandra Hotel, Pound Street, Lyme Regis, ✆ (01297) 442010, is 200 yards from the centre of town. Most bedrooms enjoy uninterrupted views out to sea, and the hotel has an unfussy, friendly atmosphere.

Connect With

Burgh Island Hotel, Bigbury-on-Sea, Devon (*see* pp.35–40).

Checklist

when to go

Although enticing for a cosy winter retreat, Dorset is lovely in **late spring and early summer**, with numerous secluded spots for picnicking and sunbathing. For the brave swimmer, the waves at Lyme Regis are at their exhilarating best during the summer.

getting there

By air: Eastleigh, Bristol, Exeter and Bournemouth international airports are all within easy travelling distance of West Dorset.

By rail: London Waterloo is 2½ hours away. Dorchester and Yeovil are the nearest stations for Summer Lodge (approximately 10 miles from either).

By car: Evershot connects with London via the A303 and M3.

booking direct

From the USA, reservations for Summer Lodge can be made through the **Relais & Châteaux** New York Sales Office, ✆ (212) 8560115.

entry formalities

US and Canadian citizens need full passports.

getting around

Car hire is recommended. Try Low Cost Transport in Dorchester, ✆ (01305) 251617, or Olds Car Rental, ✆ (01305) 266066.

getting by

The currency is the **pound sterling**. Major credit cards are accepted.

getting married

Marriages can be performed here.

England: West Sussex

Gravetye Manor
nr East Grinstead, West Sussex RH19 4LJ
☏ (01342) 810567
✉ (01342) 810080
expensive–moderate

Southeastern England, with its inclines and valleys, its chalky Downs crowned with ancient woods and its sweeping views across hills and marshy plains, unfolds gently from London down to the bracing English Channel. For newlyweds wanting to unwind for a few days before embarking on further journeys, this part of the British countryside provides both a convenient stopover and a romantic retreat. Gatwick Airport is half an hour by car from Gravetye Manor, Heathrow just an hour away—yet here, deep in West Sussex, the sense of being far removed from the 20th century prevails.

Gravetye Manor

Gravetye Manor is just 15 minutes' drive from the small market town of East Grinstead, yet it is remarkably easy to get lost in the twisting lanes and narrow roads that link it to the adjacent villages of Ardingly and Lindfield. No matter, the staff at this splendid hotel are well versed in calming down the lost and weary traveller. Call them up from what appears to be the middle of nowhere, and they will accurately and efficiently talk you right to the front door.

The approach is breathtakingly romantic. Sheltered by hills carpeted with woodland, Gravetye materializes at the end of a long, curving driveway banked with brilliant rhododendrons. Mellow-stoned and handsomely proportioned, this Elizabethan manor is overlooked by nothing—and overlooks nothing but truly English gardens and acres of forest. It is easy to lose all sense of the present within a very short space of time.

This is a hotel that is hard to fault. Yes, Gravetye has idiosyncratic touches that might annoy, but ultimately the few restrictions imposed on guests only serve to benefit all in the long run. Groups, particularly incentive groups, are discouraged, credit cards are not accepted, and notices bid drivers to park head-on, because 'Flowers Do Not Like Exhaust Fumes'. The result is a hotel where traditional values count for something, where

Gravetye Manor

quiet couples seeking peace and privacy are perhaps favoured over noisy business-folk, and where appreciation and respect for the beautiful surroundings are justifiably encouraged at all times. Fit this bill, and the rewards are high: tremendously courteous staff, cosseting and pampering at its best, delicious food, comfortable bedrooms, reading matter from the latest glossy magazines and novels to rather arcane periodicals, and chilled spring water from the estate—this is a hotel where attention to detail is obviously of paramount importance.

Private Comfort

Even the smallest **bedroom** is generously proportioned—and two of the loveliest, Walnut and Ash, are splendidly spacious. Ash, the master bedroom, is an ideal honeymooners' room. An impressive dark oak and ancient four-poster bed dominates this handsome wood-panelled room, and, in harmony with the romantic atmosphere, the wooden carved nuptial portraits of Gravetye's original owners, Richard Infield and his new bride Katharine, are set side by side above the fireplace. Like the majority of Gravetye's bedrooms, Ash has comfortable padded window-seats set in large windows overlooking the pretty gardens. In contrast to this sober if sumptuous grandeur, Ash's eccentric and fun **bathroom** is kitted out with original Art Deco fittings, spanning theatrical mirror lights, silver dolphin-shaped taps and Hollywood-style bath and basins.

Furnishings throughout are low-key and supremely tasteful, yet not so stiff and formal that guests feel inhibited about curling up in an armchair; the hotel positively inspires relaxation, and with champagne, delicious salted nuts and fruit left in the room, honeymooners are made to feel especially welcome. Paintings and drawings relate either to the Sussex countryside, flowers and plants, or to costumes from past Glyndebourne operas. Lots of thoughtful little extras keep the same guests returning. Televisions are discreetly hidden behind firescreens, there are 'his and hers' wardrobes and basins, decent-length bathrobes and plenty of luxurious bathing goodies.

Public Relaxation

The panelled public rooms are a delight: big open fires, creaking floorboards, striking floral displays and squashy sofas furnish the main **sitting room** and the outer hall; the air is rich with the smells of firewood, beeswax polish and age. Wellington boots in all sizes are lined up in a flagstoned anteroom to encourage a post-prandial turn around the magnificent **grounds**. These were originally laid out by William Robinson, the 19th-century pioneer of the English natural garden who lived at Gravetye from 1884 to 1935. In the summer, the steep banks are richly covered with flowers and shrubs, the layout appearing delightfully spontaneous. There is a **croquet lawn**, a **gazebo**, a tremendously pretty magnolia walk, and a **lake** where guests can fish for trout.

Eating In

Traditional **English** and classic **French** is the culinary theme in Gravetye's restaurant (*expensive*). The hotel's home-grown produce features on the menu: salmon, duck breasts and venison are home-smoked, and the kitchen garden allows for fresh and imaginative use of vegetables and herbs. Dishes change regularly but may include reliable favourites like *mousseline* of pike with freshwater crayfish, smoked salmon served with caviar and blinis, as well as more unusual dishes like the delicious liquorice *bavarois*. Breakfasts can be as meagre or as belt-busting as required, and similarly make use of Gravetye's own resources. The hotel's freshly pressed apple juice and conserves including home-made raspberry jam and marmalade are particularly recommended.

What to See and Do

Manor staff can organise **fishing** in the estate's 3-acre trout lake (from May through to September), as well as **golf** and **riding** nearby. The manor is surrounded by a thousand acres of forest land, and carefully mapped **walks** can be suggested.

There are also a number of **historic houses** within easy reach of the hotel.

On fine days, nearby **Wakehurst Place**, 1½ miles northwest of Ardingly on the B2028, ✆ (0181) 332 5066 (*open daily, 10–7pm in summer*), is worth visiting. Just 10 minutes' drive from Gravetye, it contains a superb collection of exotic trees and shrubs, a nature reserve and water gardens.

Petworth House and Park, ✆ (01798) 342207 (*open 1 April–end Oct, daily except Mon and Fri, 1–5.30pm*), is 45 minutes' drive away in the picturesque Sussex town of Petworth (A272). This magnificent house contains one of the most important collections of art in the country, with paintings by Turner (who used to stay at Petworth), Claude, Gainsborough, Blake and Lely. The 700-acre deer park and lake are set in grounds landscaped by Capability Brown.

The fantastical Regency froth of the **Royal Pavilion** in Brighton, ✆ (01273) *603005 (open daily 10–6pm)*, is 30 miles away, accessible via the A23. This famous seaside residence was built for George IV—it has marvellously eccentric Indian and Chinese interiors and the reconstructed kitchens, complete with tables covered with provisions and the odd mouse or two, are amusing to view.

England: Sussex

Brighton itself is an attractive seaside resort, with Regency town houses along the seafront, plenty of good restaurants, brasseries and wine bars, and a wide range of shops. During May the town stages a first-rate arts festival which attracts musicians, performers, dancers and artists from around the world, and there are plenty of concerts and exhibitions, gatherings and readings to attend (*for more information, call ✆ (01273) 676926*). The famous 'Lanes' are one of the town's biggest attractions—an area of charming cobbled alleys and passages, once home to Brighton's fishing community, and now crammed with shops selling antiques, clothes, jewellery and gifts.

Neighbouring **Lewes** (follow the A275 from East Grinstead) is an appealing market town with an ancient castle built by a follower of William the Conqueror, and picturesque medieval streets with overhanging timber-framed buildings.

Eating Out

Whytes, 33 Western Street, Brighton BN1 2PG, ✆ (01273) 776618 (*moderate*), offers assured, skilful cooking with French accent and plenty of vegetarian dishes.

Stane Street Hollow, Codmore Hill, Pulborough RH20 1BG, ✆ (01798) 872819 (*moderate–inexpensive*), is a cosy county restaurant with good-value set lunch and serious cooking throughout. The menu often features Swiss or German dishes.

Hotels Nearby

Horsted Place, Little Horsted, nr Uckfield, West Sussex TN22 5TS, ✆ 01825 750581 (*expensive–moderate*). This Victorian Gothic mansion has fine large luxurious bedrooms, pretty gardens and a reasonable restaurant.

Connect With

Westminster Hotel, Le Touquet (*see* pp.75–80).

Checklist

when to go

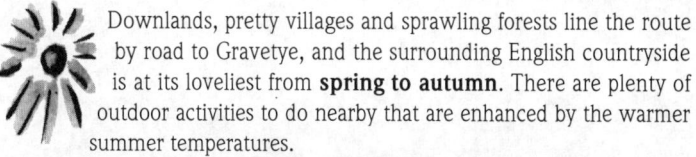

Downlands, pretty villages and sprawling forests line the route by road to Gravetye, and the surrounding English countryside is at its loveliest from **spring to autumn**. There are plenty of outdoor activities to do nearby that are enhanced by the warmer summer temperatures.

getting there

By air: Gatwick Airport is 12 miles from Gravetye; Heathrow Airport is 54 miles away.

By rail: Gatwick station is 12 miles away; London, Victoria only 30 minutes.

By car: Gravetye Manor is 30 miles from London on the M23, taking exit 10 on to the A264 towards East Grinstead. After 2 miles, at the roundabout, take 3rd exit signposted 'Haywards Heath and Brighton' (B2028).

booking direct

From the USA, reservations can be made through the **Relais & Châteaux** New York Sales Office, ✆ (212) 8560115. Single-night bookings may be refused at weekends.

entry formalities

US and Canadian citizens need full passports.

getting by

The currency is the **pound sterling**. At Gravetye Manor, no credit cards are accepted.

Fiji

Turtle Island Resort
Turtle Island, Fiji
✆ (679) 722 780
✉ (679) 665 220
expensive

Regent Hotel
Denarau Beach Resort, PO Box 9081, Nadi, Fiji
✆ (679) 750 000
✉ (679) 750 259
moderate

Fiji: Turtle Island

The 300 islands that make up the Fijian archipelago surely come very close to the city-dweller's dream of paradise, with fine sandy beaches, clear blue waters, some really first-rate hotels and resorts, superb snorkelling and diving, a distinctive cuisine and, above all, charmingly hospitable islanders. The friendliness of the Fijians is disarming. These huge, very humorous and direct people will look strangers firmly in the eye as if assessing their very essence, and if the stranger passes muster (as he or she inevitably will) then hands are clasped, arms squeezed, and even hugs will ensue. Observe Fijians within their own family environment, and you will see the importance they attach to physical contact; small children are constantly talked to, and passed from one relative to another so that their feet barely touch ground.

Fijians are also a sentimental lot. Honeymooners will receive a warm welcome, and probably won't be allowed to forget the purpose of their visit for one minute! These are islands that offer a variety of activities but are truly ideal to relax and unwind in. Bear in mind that the pace of life is incredibly slow and it is best to 'go with the flow' and start thinking Fijian time.

The Yasawa chain includes six principal islands and a number of smaller islands, all lying to the northwest of the main landmass, Viti Levu, like a string of pearls.

Nanuya Levu, better known as Turtle Island, is located in the Yasawa chain of islands; a paradise of warm blue waters, soft sands and swaying palms, made famous in the 1980 American remake of *The Blue Lagoon* featuring Brooke Shields. Turtle Island Resort is now a 500-acre, lush and jungly couples-only hideaway with accommodation in authentic but luxurious Fijian *bures* (cottages). Nearby, the Great Sea Reef offers superb diving and snorkelling.

Turtle Island Resort

About 20 years ago, a somewhat obsessive American called Richard Evanson flew to Fiji on business and, during his trip, visited Turtle Island. Evanson, though successful in his work, was unhappy in love and plagued by alcoholism. Yet he forgot his worries once he set eyes on the tiny volcanic outcrop with its gently hilly interior fringed by faultless white sand beaches.

Months later he left America and settled himself on Turtle, with just a fridge full of beer, a generator and a makeshift tent. The booze soon ran out, the tent collapsed and the generator broke down. But, undeterred and now of necessity sober, Evanson hired a young Fijian boy called Joe Naisali and together they built a shelter. That was the year that Hurricane Bébé tore through the Yasawas, blowing away both the shelter and the banyan tree to which Joe and Evanson tied themselves for safety. Amazingly, the two survived and, a little later, Columbia Pictures arrived and asked to use the island as the location for *The Blue Lagoon*. Evanson then decided to share his paradise with others and set about creating his cash-free romantic retreat. Today, both men are still very much in evidence on Turtle Island. Joe, a sturdy 40-year-old with feet the size of small skateboards, presides over all the entertainment. Richard Evanson, now with his third Fijian wife, is still sober, still obsessive, and clearly enjoys his role as the omnipresent host in his constant party of ever-changing couples.

Only heterosexuals are allowed to stay. And the couples-only rule is pretty strict—Robert Redford was turned down because he wanted to come 'as a bachelor'. But, although this insistence on coupledom evokes a somewhat sickly image of cooing newlyweds gazing all day long into each other's eyes, mercifully the reality is different. Fellow islanders tend to be a mixture of young honeymooners (often the friendliest guests) and Turtle Island returnees, mostly from Australia and America. Socializing is encouraged and guests meet each other straight away during the first-night cocktail party on the lodge terrace.

A video is made of each couple's week on the island and presented to them at the end of their stay.

Private Comfort

The island's 14 ***bures*** are strung along the principal beach among the palms and are designed so that none is overlooked by the others. With thatched roofs and windows with traditional wooden louvres, they each have two large, airy rooms, both of which have huge picture windows looking out to sea. Before guests settle in, their names are carved into a piece of driftwood which is then hung from the door. Inside, the maid has festooned the rooms with red and pink hibiscus flowers, prettily laid out on pillows, in the shower, by the washbasins and even in the lavatory!

Bure maids launder and iron clothes, and generally pamper their allocated couple. The *bure* already has a well-stocked fridge with sparkling wine (unfortunately touted as 'champagne' in the brochure), beer, water and soft drinks, but if guests want fresh fruit at 3pm each day or cheese and biscuits at midnight, then that is noted and duly supplied.

Bumper-size shampoos and conditioners line the bathroom shelves. There are books, bottles of mosquito repellent, even a couple of *sulus* or *pareos* (batik cotton wraps like sarongs) and baseball caps for day wear—on Turtle, they encourage guests to put away their home clothes as well as their cash.

Darkness falls quickly on the island and, in the evening, old-fashioned lanterns are left lit on doorsteps, so that guests can find their way to the lodge through the close-growing palm trees.

Eating In

The food is excellent and features plenty of **seafood** and salads, delicious **curries**, poppadoms and coconut rice, and sweet barbecued meats. Breakfasts include lobster omelettes and grilled swordfish and lime; all is fresh, healthy and well-balanced.

Dinner is often part of an evening's entertainment. On Lovo Night, for example, guests join in a traditional Fijian feast. The chefs wrap chicken, fish, lamb and beef in banana leaves, and these bundles are left to roast deep in the ground, on top of hot coals. The result is succulent and sweetly fragrant food which is served **buffet**-style with salads. After dinner, the staff entertain with 'Meke', songs about Fijian history, legends and love, followed by traditional spear dances. The men dress in full warrior costume and the women wear colourful *sulus*.

On some evenings, everyone on the island climbs to the top of the highest mountain for a sunset **barbecue.** As darkness falls and the Southern Cross illuminates the sky, all present are encouraged to form a 'cone of silence', with eyes closed, listening to the night sounds in the cool breeze.

For the rest of the week, the choice is between taking meals *en famille* around a long dining-table set out in the open on the terrace, or as a couple in some quiet spot, perhaps overlooking the lagoon with just the clear moon and a lantern to light the evening. This is a romantic notion that works well. Couples enjoy picking out some remote part of the island; their table, complete with fine linen and silver cutlery, champagne and candles, can even be set on the walkway which spans the mangrove swamp.

What to See and Do

On Turtle Island there is a beach for every couple, one of which is aptly named Honeymoon Beach: a sandy, secluded cove with a thatched shelter and double hammock. All the sights and landmarks of the island are pointed out on your initial **boat trip.**

Passing Paddy's Island and Devil's Rock, the boat reaches a sparkling lagoon where silvery shoals of sardines jump over the gentle ripples left by the wake. Herons observe the proceedings from the seclusion of the mangrove walkway. And when the boat reaches the **Blue Lagoon**, Joe Naisali asks if anyone is thirsty. On cue, a picnic basket filled with bottles of icily fresh papaya juice 'magically' floats up to the boat. This is a typical Turtle Island trick; the staff anticipate and satisfy guests' every need with playful glee.

The rate on Turtle Island is all-inclusive, payable in advance 8 weeks before the start of the holiday, and plenty of watersports and activities are provided for guests as part of the package. Couples can **snorkel** over exquisitely colourful coral in the morning, when they are dropped on their chosen private beach for a **swim** and a **sunbathe**. At a pre-arranged time, one of the staff will arrive by motorboat and set up a picnic lunch (the menu chosen by the couple that morning) on the sands. Other activities include **deep-sea fishing, canoeing, scuba diving, tennis** and **horse riding** and the island is easy and interesting to **walk** around.

A number of half-day excursions are also available. On Sundays, the launch takes guests over to **Matacawalevu**, the largest neighbouring island, where you can join in the Sunday service at the Methodist church. This offers a tremendously rewarding insight into Fijian life. The children, dressed in their Sunday best, are clearly delighted to meet foreigners. They giggle in the aisles, stare unashamedly and take no notice of the 'hellfire and brimstone' sermon. Like their parents, they clearly enjoy the communal hymn singing.

Further along the island, at **Vuaki**, is the Catholic village, another simple arrangement of *bures*, a church and a school. Here, visitors can sit in on a school lesson, as well as pay a visit to Cheif Ratu Emosi's *bure*.

For their honeymoon, one couple decided to try something adventurous—a sailing holiday around the Fijian islands. 'I wasn't very keen at first,' confessed the bride, 'but I was talked into it. He wanted to do something active rather than sitting on a beach all day.' Unfortunately the groom began to suffer from chronic seasickness, had to be put ashore—and the bride decided to sail away with the others. 'I was having a really good time,' she said apologetically, 'and we'd spent all that money...' The groom spent the next 10 days alone, doing just what he'd hoped to avoid: sitting on a beach...

Turtle Island: What to See and Do

Fiji: Viti Levu

Around a hundred of the islands of the Fijian archipelago are inhabited; the largest at roughly 10,300 square kilometres is Viti Levu, home to about 70 per cent of the population. Vanua Levu in the northeast is the second-largest island. The others are scattered throughout 500,000 square kilometres of the southwest Pacific Ocean and are divided into named groups—Yasawa, Lau, Kadavu and Lomaiviti.

Viti Levu's capital and port is Suva, to the southeast of the island, but it is on the sunny leeward or western coast that one finds most of the holiday resorts. On this coast skies are generally clearer, and breezes help to keep the temperatures at a tolerable level. The resorts here are also within minutes of Nadi (pronounced Nandi), the site of Fiji's international airport.

Navsori Highlands

Regent Hotel

The Regent, on the private island of Denarau in Nadi Bay, is one of the best hotels in the archipelago. Here guests can find a wholly individual, vibrantly ethnic atmosphere, without loss of luxurious trimmings. It is laid out in the manner of a traditional Fijian village, with the village 'dwellings', two-storey wood-constructed bedrooms and suites, encircling the principal buildings. In place of the village church one finds a vast and breezy open-air lobby and lounge with a huge, vaulted ceiling. Nearby are the shops and beyond them the bars and restaurants. And surrounding these are delightfully tropical gardens, lush and rich with exotic frangipani, red ginger, hibiscus and crotons, the floral ingredients for the traditional welcome garlands known as *salusalus*. There is also a living arts complex where wood carvings, pottery, paintings and artefacts made by local artists are displayed.

Private Comfort

Each of the 285 **rooms**, including the 6 **beachfront suites** feature private verandahs with mesmerically lovely views over the Pacific. There is air-conditioning too, and furnishings in rooms and suites are attractively ethnic in style, with use of patterned batik, rattan, quarry tiles, strong dark colours and natural wood. Traditional cotton robes are provided as cool cover-ups after sunbathing. It is also worth investing in a colourful cotton sarong; the hotel's shop sells a wide range at affordable prices.

The *Fiji Times* is brought with breakfast, 'The First Newspaper Published In The World Today' splashed across its front page. This impressive-sounding claim can be made because the island is so near to the International Date Line.

Public Relaxation

The hotel has a large **swimming pool** with a swim-up bar next to the beach, and there are 8 **restaurants** and **lounges** dotted throughout the resort. Some, like the open-air **Meke Lounge** that overlooks the pool, are given over to early evening entertainment (*5.30–6.30pm*) when drinks are discounted; there is live music and dancing, and free snacks.

What to See and Do

Days at the Regent can be spent **fishing, waterskiing, snorkelling, parasailing** or **jet-skiing**. A fee is charged for these watersports, though hobiecats, windsurfing, paddle boats and beginners' lessons are free.

In the evening, hotel entertainments include Fijian storytelling, sadly a poorly attended event. Even if it ends up as a 'one-to-one' chat, this can be a rewarding experience; Katerina, the storyteller, is as happy to gossip about the local government and the problems of disciplining flirtatious Fijian girls as she is to discuss the significance of whales' teeth.

There are a variety of theme-nights each week. The villagers of Yanuca 'firewalk' on Wednesdays; there are regular Chinese buffets and Magiti feasts, during which Fijian foods are cooked in a *lovo*, or underground oven; and Mekes (entertainment featuring traditional songs and dances). But perhaps most memorable of all is the dusk torch-lighting ceremony. Flames lit by traditionally dressed 'warriors' illuminate both beach and sky while the wooden *lalis*, or native drums, announce the setting of the sun.

Day trips on and around Viti Levu concentrate on the western side of the island. The Regent has details of trips, as does the tourist magazine *Fiji Magic*, which is available in shops, the airport and hotel bedrooms. South Sea Cruises, ✆ 722 988, offers 4-island **sightseeing cruises** with pick-ups from all the Nadi hotels. They visit Castaway Island, Musket Cove, Plantation Island and Mana Island, all of which are 'resort islands' just off the western coast, with great beaches and good snorkelling in clear, safe waters.

The **Garden of the Sleeping Giant**, ✆ 722 701 (*open daily; admission F$8.50*), about 5km from Nadi airport at the foot of the Sabeto Mountains, is famed for its collection of 30–40 different Asian orchids and hybrids, its jungly gardens and canopied boardwalk through fantastic landscaped grounds and lily ponds. The garden once belonged to the burly American actor, Raymond Burr, who made his name playing TV detectives Perry Mason and Ironside.

Viseisei, about 9km north of Nadi, is the oldest village on the island. There is a crafts centre, a chief's *bure*, and a large Methodist church with a monument commemorating the arrival of the missionaries.

To escape the tourist trail head north along the coastal route known as the **King's Road**. This area is less developed than other parts of Viti Levu and the scenery is tremendously beautiful, but caution is needed when driving (4-wheel-drive vehicles are best). Inland from the market town of **Tavua**, which is about 90 km north along the coast from Nadi airport, is **Navala**, a pretty mountain village of thatched homes. Just south of Navala, the gold-mining settlement of **Vatukoula** is one of the last bastions of colonialism in Fiji; the local club, golf course and bowling green are still kept in pristine condition.

Suva, the capital in the southeast of the island, is well worth a visit, and can easily be explored on foot within a day, but it is always either very muggy or wet. The colourful municipal market stocks a heady array of Indian spices, fresh exotic fruits, Indian snacks and shellfish. Behind the post office on Stinson Street is a handicraft centre selling woodcarving, *masi* cloth, necklaces and batik clothing. Cumming Street has good restaurants and duty-free shops, and the **Fiji Museum** in Thurston Gardens (*open daily except Sunday*) stages good exhibitions on the history of the islands and islanders.

Eating Out

Curry Restaurant, Clay Street, Nadi (*inexpensive*), serves delicious local curries.

Tiko's Restaurant, Suva Harbour, near Victoria Parade, ℂ 313 626 (*moderate–inexpensive*). Suva's floating restaurant, Tiko's, was featured in the 1980 film *The Blue Lagoon*. Fijian seafood specialities served here include prawns and clams cooked in coconut milk.

Hotels Nearby

Yasawa Island Lodge, PO Box 10128, Nadi Airport, Fiji, ℂ (679) 663 364 (*expensive*), is a romantic island resort with 16 beachfront *bures*.

Checklist

when to go

Fiji has a tropical climate, tempered by trade winds. Weather conditions do vary from island group to island group, though there is a tendency towards humidity throughout the archipelago. The cool, dry months are **May to October**, with temperatures dropping during **July and August** to a pleasant 18–20°C.

getting there

International air carriers flying to Nadi International Airport include Air New Zealand, Qantas, Canadian Airlines International and Japan Airlines.

From the UK: There are scheduled flights with Air New Zealand to Nadi Airport (via Los Angeles). Most guests who book with The Travel Portfolio stay overnight at the Regent.

From the USA: Scheduled flights with Qantas or Air New Zealand depart from Los Angeles, San Francisco and Vancouver B.C.

A return seaplane transfer from Nadi to Turtle Island takes 30 minutes and costs £528 per couple. Luggage allowance is one 40lb suitcase per person.

tour operators

Airwaves, 10 Bective Place, London SW15 2PZ, ✆ (0181 875 1188), handles reservations for the Regent.

Reservations for Turtle must be for a minimum of 6 nights. From the UK, bookings can be made through the **Travel Portfolio Ltd**, 73 Churchgate Street, Bury St Edmunds IP33 1RL, ✆ (01284) 700444, 📠 (01284) 769011.

From the USA, reservations can be made through **Turtle Holidays**, Quad 205 Bldg A-1, 10906 N.E. 39th Street, Vancouver, WA 98682-6789, toll-free ✆ (800) 826 3083, ✆ (206) 256 4347, 📠 (206) 253 3934.

booking direct

Reservations for the Regent can be made through **Four Seasons & Regent**: from the UK, freefone ✆ (0800) 282 245; and from the USA, toll-free ✆ (800) 545 4000.

entry formalities

UK, US and Canadian citizens need full passports and return tickets.

health

Immunization against cholera, typhoid, polio and hepatitis A is recommended. Sterilize drinking water.

getting around

Car rental is relatively cheap, and most of the major rental companies are represented at Nadi Airport. A 4-wheel-drive vehicle is recommended if you want to explore the wilder north of the island. The Regent is 10 minutes' drive from the airport.

getting by

Fijian, **Hindi** and **English** are the 3 main languages of Fiji. The currency is the **Fijian dollar**. Major credit cards are accepted. On Turtle, no **currency** is needed since everything is pre-paid with the balance due 8 weeks before departure.

getting married

The Regent will stage Fijian-style weddings with traditional costume and music. On Turtle Island, couples can marry in a traditional Fijian wedding ceremony. Catholic and Methodist clergy are available, along with a Fijian church choir.

France: Côte d'Azur

Grand-Hotel du Cap Ferrat
06230 Saint-Jean-Cap-Ferrat, France
✆ (33) 93 76 50 50
✉ (33) 93 76 04 52
expensive

If your choice of a honeymoon location has narrowed down to a European resort with not too many high-rise hotels, an inviting clear blue sea and a certain touch of glamour and grandeur, however faded, then the Côte d'Azur should fit the bill. With its three Corniches running alongside the limpid Mediterranean and providing breathtaking views of pretty fishing ports, this rocky coastline has played host to hordes of famous honeymooners over the years. It's still a shamelessly romantic venue—even the obligatory sex kittens frolicking hopefully on the beaches of Cannes add to its air of raffish charm. And though the hillsides which hug the coast have become increasingly built-up, the region remains richly tropical in appearance. Despite being a rich man's paradise, Cap Ferrat is a serenely unspoilt part of the French Riviera, with wild umbrella pines, craggy sheltered coves and sweet-smelling wildflowers giving balance to the imposing and sometimes monstrous-looking holiday villas.

Grand-Hotel du Cap Ferrat

The Grand-Hotel du Cap Ferrat has many of the essential ingredients for a perfect honeymoon hotel: comfort, pampering, a friendly atmosphere—plus the sense of being special. An elegant creamy-white Edwardian pile, it also enjoys a spectacular setting, at the apex of the rocky pine-green peninsula of Cap Ferrat.

Private Comfort

Bedrooms are blissfully old fashioned: cream-panelled and airy, with comfortable big beds, French windows overlooking the sea, and fabulous marble **bathrooms** with fluffy bathrobes, myriad upmarket pungent unctions, as well as power showers and separate loos. In the morning you can have breakfast brought to your room or, better still, take it out on the terrace sheltered by pine trees (also the setting for lunch and dinner), which looks over the formal gardens to the sea beyond.

Public Relaxation

The hotel has a grand and spacious **lobby**, made grander by impressive antiques, enormous flower displays, somewhat intimidating chi-chi boutiques and numerous overstuffed sofas. There are 'jump-to-it' bell hops dressed in natty grey cropped jackets with matching trousers, uncannily similar to the delicate illustrations of smartly dressed waiters or hotel staff you might find in a *Tintin* or *Babar* children's book. Yet for such a grand hotel the staff are enormously friendly, quick to smile hello or comply with the most infra-dig of requests. If your budget means you have to ask about the regularity of the local buses rather than the reliability of the local limo service, the receptionist's expression will remain impressively neutral.

The dress code during the day is informal. Most guests head for the hotel's own **beach club**, the Club Dauphin across the road, which fronts a rocky bay (like much of the Côte d'Azur, there is no sandy beach). You can either walk there along a zigzagging pathway, which leads you down through delightful gardens punctuated by perfectly sculpted cypresses, or take the hotel's **funicular railway**. The Club Dauphin has an open-air **poolside restaurant** for informal lunches, and drinks are brought to your side at the mere click of a finger. For lazy days, lie back in a sumptuously comfortable recliner, a cool beer to hand, and admire the mesmerising stream of mega-yachts swishing across the bay. This club is so relaxed that even the few children present fall asleep! It also boasts a truly first-rate heated seawater **swimming pool**, Olympic in size, and designed to give the uncanny illusion of water falling away into the ocean beyond.

Eating In

In the evenings guests dress up in preparation for 'Le Grand Bouffe'. Start with a glass of champagne on the terrace accompanied by irresistible roasted almonds, and the tinkle of well-played Chopin from the Somerset Maugham piano bar. You may only be able to afford to eat at the hotel once, for *cappuccinos* work out at around £6 a cup, and the cheapest set menu comes priced at 390F—but it will be worth it. Chef Jean-Claude Guillon tempts the taste-buds with exotic delicacies like freshwater langoustines, St Pierre fish (John Dory) with spinach, succulent lamb served with polenta and beans, and superb puddings from mini crème brulées to fresh fruit sorbets. The waiters and *maître d'* are genuinely charming, and deeply concerned if you find yourself too full to manage more than 3 courses.

What to See and Do

Cap Ferrat has a dramatic coastal path that you can walk around quite easily. From the Club Dauphin, the eastbound cliff path takes you to the old fishing town of **St-Jean-Cap-Ferrat** within 30 minutes. With its postcard-pretty harbour, good cafés and restaurants and small town hall boasting a *salle des mariages* decorated by Jean Cocteau, it is worth visiting. The longer (2-hour) and more energetic stroll westwards takes you towards Villefranche-sur-Mer, one of the most sheltered of Mediterranean harbours. The views at every turn are achingly lovely Monet-style *tableaux vivants*, featuring intense turquoise-clear sea in sheltered coves (colonised early in the day by naturists, picnickers and French families), dramatically sheer cliff-faces topped with umbrella pines and, beyond, the rooftops of Villefranche. At the end of the walk is the Cap's only sandy beach at **Plage de Passable** along the chemin du Roy.

The interior of the Cap is a pretty latticework of well-tended hedge-lined avenues, interrupted by grand wrought-iron gates concealing unfeasibly large holiday homes belonging to the rich and famous. Somerset Maugham lived at the Villa Mauresque and Sir Andrew Lloyd Webber and his wife Madeleine have a home close to the lighthouse with enviably uncluttered views out to the sea. On wet days, visit the pink-toned Italianate **Villa Ephrussi de Rothschild**, ✆ 93 01 33 09 (*open daily 10–6pm; 7pm July–Aug*), situated on the upper part of Cap Ferrat. Once the home of the colourful Madame Beatrice de Rothschild, who travelled everywhere with a trunk full of assorted wigs, the villa now houses the Musée Ile-de-France, and boasts a fine collection of 18th-century paintings, furniture and *objets d'art*. The 7 gardens are geographically themed, with Spanish, Italian, Florentine and Japanese sections, and on a clear day you can see all the way from Villefranche to the Italian border.

By contrast, **Villefranche-sur-Mer** with its narrow alleys, its pink, yellow and red stucco houses packed against the hillside and its busy little harbour provides a taste of real life. There is a sheltered beach, a variety of friendly quayside bars, cafés and restaurants, and an interesting range of souvenir and clothes shops.

'Menton's dowdy, Monte's brass, Nice is rowdy, Cannes is class'—the old twenties rhyme still has some truth in it but, given that 3 of these resorts are easily accessible from Cap Ferrat, it's worth checking them out in order to form your own opinion. **Menton** has an old quarter which is well worth visiting. Steep and narrow cobbled lanes flanked by tiny cottages form a labyrinth around the hilltop cathedral, and the ochre and burnt sienna façades give the quarter a decidedly Italian air. Menton's town hall also has a Cocteau-decorated *salle des mariages* depicting various romantic scenes. And of course **Monte Carlo**, though somewhat spoilt by skyscrapers, remains a sophisticated resort. Its elaborate Baroque-style casino, mimicking a rich and glorious wedding cake, still throngs with life during the evenings—and if you can tear yourselves away from the gaming tables a trip to the pretty yet primly pristine principality of Monaco should amuse. The **Prince's Palace** (*open June–Oct*), though still occupied by Prince Rainier and his family, has public rooms which contain a priceless collection of paintings by such artists as Titian, Breughel and Van Loo, as well as royal portraits. The palace is accessible by bus or taxi; parking is severely restricted on the Monaco Rock. In **Nice**, visit the old town—you can enter from the seaside at the quai des Etats-Unis or from the main bus station—and make a point of strolling through the charming afternoon flower market at the cours Saleya. The air is heady with the scent of roses, tulips, dahlias and geraniums, and the square is surrounded by cafés, pizza stalls and cheapish bistros.

Eating Out

Given the staggering cost of eating at the Grand-Hotel du Cap Ferrat, it is well worth moving further afield for lunches and dinners. There are popular restaurants, cafés and snack bars facing the harbour at St Jean-Cap-Ferrat.

Le Rafiot, ✆ 93 76 01 14 (*moderate*), is one definitely to try, where seafood from char-grilled crayfish to fish soup with *rouille*, is eaten on the outside terrace.

Lou Roucas, quai Courbet, Villefranche-sur-Mer, ✆ 93 01 90 12 (*inexpensive*), is a friendly sea-facing restaurant where you can enjoy simple set lunches which include wine. Incredibly good value in this category.

Hotels Nearby

**Hotel Clair Logis, 12 avenue centrale, 06230 St-Jean-Cap-Ferrat, ✆ 93 76 04 57 (*cheap*), is an old fashioned villa set in peaceful parkland.

***Welcome, quai Admiral Courbet, Villefranche-sur-Mer, ✆ 93 76 76 93 (*moderate*). This hotel has air-conditioned rooms, the most appealing of which are located on the fifth floor.

Hotel Lancaster, Paris (see pp.69–74).

Westminster Hotel, Le Touquet (*see* pp.75–80).

Connect With

*****Hotel Splendido, Portofino, Italy (*see* pp.103–108).

Checklist

when to go

The climate is reliably warm during the spring, and mostly bearable in summer months. **May and September** are ideal months to visit: resorts are less crowded and hotel rates are lower; at the Grand, rates drop dramatically in March, April, November and December.

getting there

By air: Nice International Airport is 25 minutes from the hotel by limousine transfer or taxi. Smaller airlines tend to have better-value fares or special deals, for instance British Midland, who fly daily to Nice from Heathrow, and twice weekly from East Midlands Airport. For reservations, freefone ✆ (0345) 554554. Most major international carriers, including British Airways and Air France, fly regularly to Nice from all other major European destinations.

tour operators

In the UK, **Elegant Resorts**, The Old Palace, Chester CH1 1RB, ✆ (01 244) 897 777, have week-long packages to the Grand-Hotel du Cap Ferrat, inclusive of return flights and limousine transfer; a 3-night honeymoon package is also available.

booking direct

From the USA, reservations can be made through **RMI Marketing**, toll-free ✆ (800) 225 4255; in New York, call ✆ (212) 696 4566. Reservations can also be made through the **Relais & Châteaux** New York Sales Office, ✆ (212) 8560115.

entry formalities

US and Canadian citizens need full passports; a British Visitor's Passport is valid for stays of up to 3 months.

getting around

Taxis are incredibly expensive, and buses unreliable, so **car** hire is very strongly recommended. Major car rental companies are represented at Nice Airport. It is worth investigating the cost of pre-booked car hire from the UK, since local deals are unlikely to be cheaper.

getting by

The currency is the **French franc**. Take travellers' cheques or Eurocheques. Major credit cards are accepted.

France: Côte d'Azur

France: Paris

Hotel Lancaster
7 rue de Berri, 75008 Paris, France
✆ (331) 40 76 40 76
✉ (331) 40 76 40 00
expensive

By tradition the city of lovers, Paris can be a celebration of all that is life-enhancing. In this most sensual of cities, walking slowly along the banks of the River Seine hand in hand is considered neither foolish nor sentimental; enjoying a long, leisurely gourmet lunch is the accepted norm. Equally, sitting for hours in a pavement café watching the world go by is seen as a beneficial pursuit rather than a waste of time. Moreover, since it is easy to escape the crowds as well as to explore much of Paris on foot, the pace of life is relaxed.

And the city's sheer beauty rarely fails to move. It is easy to understand why Paris attracts artists. A model of architectural planning, it is also relatively free from modern eyesores.

The Left Bank, with its narrow streets, tempting shops, street markets and restaurants, is picturesque; at its heart, and floating mid-stream in the Seine, the two 'islands' of St Louis and la Cité are tranquil miniature communities.

Hotel Lancaster

The Hotel Lancaster is very well placed for sightseeing. Located just off the Champs-Élysées, in the narrow rue de Berri, it is within walking distance of the Eiffel Tower, the Louvre, the Seine and the Lido, as well as famous shops and department stores. Despite its central location, it is a cosy, intimate townhouse hotel, a true hideaway—unmodernised but thoroughly renovated, with a tremendously romantic courtyard garden. It is also charmingly decorated throughout, with 18th-century antiques and *objets d'art*.

Built in 1899, The Lancaster became a hotel in the twenties. Its founder, Emile Wolf, used to boast, 'I don't have clients, I have only friends,' a credo he carried through, not only in the elegant yet home-like furnishings, but also in his patronage of the Russian artist Boris Pastoukhoff. Wolf filled his hotel with Pastoukhoff's canvases in lieu of payment from the artist for board and lodgings.

Private Comfort

The atmosphere remains very much that of an elegant private home, and if a suite is affordable it will be well worth the extra expense. The 10 **suites** have pretty sitting rooms with cream-coloured panelling, log fires, books, magazines and oil-paintings, comfortable sofas, television and hi-fi. Day beds and Art Deco **bathrooms** enhance the individuality of these rooms—one even houses a grand piano, and all have secluded **balconies** embellished with flower-filled window-boxes. Those located in the 'attic' enjoy good views over the famous grey slate rooftops of Paris, towards the Eiffel Tower and Sacré-Cœur beyond. Breakfasts are truly indulgent affairs, and can be served on guests' balconies in good weather. It is almost impossible to resist this mouthwatering collation of warm *pain-au-chocolat*, sticky *pain-au-raisin* fresh from the oven, sweet freshly squeezed orange juice, and strong, fortifying coffee.

Public Relaxation

Public areas are intimate and welcoming. The concierge's desk is as tiny as a theatre box and just as ornate, and on one side of the lobby there is a bar that looks more like a cosy English sitting room. The courtyard, formerly the coaching house and stables, with its profusion of trellises covered with ivy, honeysuckle and columbine, its bronze statuary of frolicking putti and its charming wrought-iron furniture, is a peaceful venue for cocktails and summer breakfasts.

Eating In

The small, smart restaurant serves **traditional French** cuisine and has an excellent and lengthy wine list.

What to See and Do

The museums, monuments and art galleries of Paris are well documented and rewarding to visit. Just as appealing are the many romantic hidden *quartiers*, with some of the prettiest parts of Paris found within the **Left Bank**.

The best way to explore this artistic quarter is on foot, starting at the 12th-century church of St-Germain des Prés. The boulevard St-Germain is home to celebrated cafés, like La Coupole, Le Flore (where Jean-Paul Sartre and Simone de Beauvoir set up literary shop during the Second World War), and Les Deux Magots—still redolent of the ghosts of Mallarmé, Gide and Hemingway. As many locals as tourists patronise their pavement tables; prices are high, but lingering is allowed.

The villagey atmosphere of the Left Bank is at its strongest in the tiny streets and squares that back on to the boulevard. The enchanting square off the rue du Furstemberg is where the painter Delacroix had his studio; the rue Jacob is full of interesting antiques shops, and the pretty rue de Seine has a colourful fruit, flower and vegetable market.

The **Right Bank** covers a much greater area and, with its wide avenues built by Baron Haussmann, is less intimate in scale, more stately in atmosphere. The old marketplace of Les Halles has become a magnet for tourists, trend-setters and mime artists. The controversial landmark of the **Centre Pompidou**, designed by the British architect Richard Rogers, stages interesting art exhibitions and there are great views over Paris from its skeletal external escalators.

Hidden havens exist even on the Right Bank and include parts of **Montmartre** and the **Marais**, stretching west to east between Les Halles and the Bastille. Full of elegant townhouses, boutiques, contemporary art galleries, salons and designer shops, this is a visually appealing, trendy and yet relatively peaceful quarter. At its heart is the beautiful 17th-century **Place des Vosges**: an imposing square of 36 red-hued and stone-faced houses with steep pitched roofs and arcaded ground floors which surround a garden of fountains and pretty trees. Eccentric shops, old-fashioned bars and small restaurants can be found around the square.

Eating Out

Le Polidor, 41 rue Monsieur le Prince, 75006, ✆ 43 26 95 34 (*inexpensive*), is an atmospheric bistro, serving good, basic, French fare; very popular.

Chartier, 7 rue du Faubourg-Montmartre, 75009, ✆ 4 70 86 29 (*inexpensive*). An enormous, lively Art Nouveau brasserie, Chartier is very good value within this category. Queuing and sharing tables is mandatory.

Chez Paul, 13 rue de Charonne, 75011, ✆ 47 00 34 57 (*moderate*). This revamped old bistro serves traditional dishes; it is particularly popular with the artistic community.

Hotels Nearby

Relais Christine, 3 rue Christine, ✆ 43 26 71 80 (*expensive–moderate*), is a pretty, converted 16th-century monastery with a garden and a courtyard, attractively decorated bedrooms and a friendly atmosphere.

Hotel de la Place des Vosges, 12 rue de Birague, 75004, ✆ 42 72 60 46 (*moderate*). This is a charming 17th-century townhouse in a quiet location.

Connect With

Grand-Hotel du Cap Ferrat, St-Jean-Cap-Ferrat (*see* pp.63–68).
Westminster Hotel, Le Touquet (*see* pp.75–80).

Checklist

when to go

Paris enjoys a mild climate, and **spring** is traditionally the favoured time for visitors, though any month throughout the year brings its charms to this city. It can get hot and muggy in August, which is why this is the month when the majority of Parisians escape to the country or seaside.

getting there

By air: Major European and American carriers fly direct to Roissy (Charles-de-Gaulle) airport. Taxi rides from the airport can be costly; however, there is an Air France airport bus which leaves every 20 minutes for the Arc de Triomphe or nearby Porte Maillot (journey time around 30 minutes). Taxi connections can be made there, though the Hotel Lancaster is only 10 minutes' walk from the Arc de Triomphe.

By rail: From the UK the Eurostar high-speed train travels from Waterloo Station in London to the heart of Paris in about 3 hours (Hotel Lancaster offers affordable 2-night Eurostar packages). The nearest Métro station is Charles-de-Gaulle-Etoile.

entry formalities

US and Canadian citizens need full passports; a British Visitor's Passport is valid for stays of up to 3 months.

getting around

Taxis are reasonably priced; the **Metro** is user-friendly and very good value for money.

getting by

The currency is the **French franc**. Major credit cards are accepted.

Paris: Checklist

France: Le Touquet

The Westminster Hotel
Avenue du Verger, 62520 Le Touquet, France
℡ (33) 21 05 48 48
✆ (33) 21 05 45 45
expensive–moderate

A stay at the French seaside resort of Le Touquet combines well with a British-based honeymoon, and is ideal for couples wanting a peaceful contrast to a stimulating week in Paris. It is also perfect on its own, for a long weekend visit. With its wide sandy beaches, tempting fish restaurants, exuberantly designed holiday villas and somewhat raffish elegance, Le Touquet is a typical north-coast resort.

Sporting activities play a major role in the life of the town, both for visitors and residents. These range from horse-riding, tennis, golf and windsurfing through to sand-yachting. There is a large thalassotherapy centre for those wishing to be pampered the French way, as well as inland villages and towns nearby for sightseeing.

Le Touquet lies some 20 miles from the ferry port of Boulogne, but honeymooners travelling from England have the more interesting option of flying in five-seater Piper Senecas from the quaintly old-fashioned airport at Biggin Hill (see p.80). Feeling more like a friendly suburban golf club than an airport, it even serves home-made scones, gin and tonics and tea 'like mother makes' in its cosy café. Five tiny planes do the Le Touquet run with the aptly named private carrier company of Love Air, and, cruising at only 2500 feet, the 40-minute journey also provides a rare opportunity for viewing the green and gentle Kent countryside at close quarters. Cows, sheep, stately homes, forests and vividly coloured patchwork fields are all clearly visible from the plane.

Westminster Hotel

The Westminster Hotel is located in the heart of Le Touquet and is just 5 minutes' walk from the seafront. This Art Deco hotel, with its pink brick façade interrupted by curved bay windows, faces the forest on one side and Le Touquet town on the other. There are some appealing Art Deco touches throughout the hotel, the centrepiece of which is the stylish, delicate filigree wrought-ironwork, used both on the grille of the antique wooden lifts and in the sweeping expanse of the Hollywood-style staircase.

Private Comfort

Bedrooms are generously proportioned, the larger ones face the forest and include a lobby entrance and sitting area. The decoration is subdued, indeed almost austere in parts, with subtle cream and lavender-grey colour schemes, huge thirties-style day-beds dressed in cream-coloured drapes, king-sized beds and the barest minimum of paintings or ornaments. In some ways this unfussy approach to décor mirrors the no-nonsense style of 'luxury' hotels in Eastern Europe; right through to authentically Art Deco **bathrooms**, seemingly untouched over the years, with their emphasis on plain tiling, black linoleum and chrome fixtures and fittings.

The **honeymoon room** (160F) at the Westminster, all cream drapes swept up into dramatic swags over a massive bed and the window-frame and featuring crafted walnut furniture and subtle lighting, is appealing in a cinematic way—and well worth booking in advance for that extra touch of romantic glamour. Flowers and champagne are left in the room if requested beforehand.

Public Relaxation

There is a good-sized **swimming pool**, **steam** and **sauna rooms**, **snooker**, a comfortable **bar**, serving a wide variety of champagnes as well as cocktails, and a **coffee shop** for brasserie-style buffet lunches and dinners.

Eating In

Le Pavillon restaurant serves gastronomic dinners. Breakfast is a continental buffet and, at 75F, does not represent good value for money. Unless it is included in the price of a package, it is better to skip this and have breakfast at one of the many cosy cafés off the rue St-Jean.

What to See and Do

Le Touquet was popularised as a resort in the late 19th century by a couple of Parisian newspaper magnates, and much of the town was built subsequently, during the 1920s. Intended as a sort of 'Cannes du Nord', the town is set out in a neat grid-like format of super-straight avenues, manicured squares and controlled forest. This makes it easy to explore on foot, yet at the same time lends the place a slight air of toytown unreality. Flowers fill the tiny gardens of every villa, grow abundantly in the rich soil borders running alongside the pavements, and spill out of ubiquitous hanging baskets and balconies. The powder-soft sand covering the wide expanse of beach looks clean, combed and well cared for.

In one small street alone, it is quite normal to come across a vastly diverse array of architectural oddities: miniature Gothic-style turrets topping tiny holiday villas, or the steeply pitched gabled roof of a Swiss chalet, while across the road stands a mansion built in the Normandy manner, all stripy wood and shuttered windows. On the corner of the avenue Edward VII stands a fabulously flamboyant Gothic

town hall, housing a library stocked with English novels which even the temporary visitor can borrow for a day or so. The polychromatic brick Catholic church of **Jeanne d'Arc**, which stands opposite the town hall, can be booked by foreign protestants wishing to marry in Le Touquet. Just bring a vicar along and the denomination changes automatically. The early settlers called Le Touquet 'Paris-Plage', and the sobriquet has stuck. Many of the fantastical homes are the holiday retreats of rich Parisians. But it was also the English who helped to put Le Touquet on the map. During the twenties and thirties, they came in search of golf and gambling; the Prince of Wales was a frequent visitor, as was Noël Coward and also P.G. Wodehouse, who made his home in the town's forest area.

Today, **golf** is still a passion with visitors: there are 2 9-hole courses, with an 18-hole course about to be completed on the edge of the forest. A really impressive **Equestrian Centre** is located on the avenue de la Dune aux Loups, ✆ 21 05 15 25, with 260 stalls and facilities for group rides in the forest and on the beach. On the avenue de l'Hippodrome there are facilities for **archery** and **clay pigeon shooting**, together with a large sports centre housing all-weather **tennis** courts. On the seafront, visitors can sign up for **sailing, boating, jet-skiing, windsurfing** and **sand-surfing**. Most hotels will arrange sporting facilities for guests, or call the Sports Office, ✆ 21 05 21 65. A *Carte Sport Pour Tous* costs 60F and allows holders to practise a number of different sports at a discounted rate.

Le Touquet's **beach**, with its faultless and broad expanse of sand, is understandably very popular with sand-yachters, sunbathers and swimmers. At the end of the rue St-Jean is **Aqualud**, ✆ 21 05 63 59, billed as Europe's largest swimming pool. This glass-domed edifice houses a watery oasis of labyrinthine slides, miniature pools and jacuzzis, and is kept at a constantly agreeable temperature all year round.

The rue St-Jean and the rue de Metz are Le Touquet's main **shopping** streets. Good fashion stores mix with tempting *traiteurs* and *chocolatiers*—and the mesmerising Marché Couvert (*open Mon, Thurs and Sat*), a third of the way down the rue de Metz, is a Mecca of take-home gastronomic goodies. Mouthwatering terrines and sweet and savoury tarts are lined up alongside home-made myrtle jams; rows of tiny goat's cheeses share stall-space with ripe tomatoes still on the vine, shiny gooseberries, plump strawberries and raspberries. For picnic lunches, the range of ready-cooked food is immensely appealing, with stuffed pancakes, quiches, chicken Madras and *paella*, and ready-to-eat *fruits-de-mer*.

Out of town, **Montreuil** (10 miles from Le Touquet, take the D143), is worth a visit. This medieval hilltop town with its ruined citadel is where Victor Hugo set parts of *Les Miserables*. **Boulogne** (20 miles from town) has an interesting historical centre, good shops and restaurants and a lively market.

Eating Out

Château de Montreuil, 4 chaussée des Capuchins, 62170 Montreuil, ⊘ 21 81 53 04 (*expensive*). A Relais & Châteaux establishment, this lovely large old house with its walled garden has been awarded two Gault Millau *toques*. The chefs are Roux-brothers trained.

Chez Perard, 67 rue de Metz, ⊘ 21 05 13 33 (*moderate*). A popular and unpretentious fish restaurant with live music, Chez Perard offers an enormous *plateau de fruits-de-mer* of lobsters, crayfish, crabs, oysters and prawns served up in a miniature rowing boat.

Café de la Forêt, place de l'Hermitage, ⊘ 21 05 01 05 (*inexpensive*), is an informal brasserie–restaurant within a casino complex. The set menus are from 98F.

Hotels Nearby

Auberge de la Grenouillère, La Madeleine-sous-Montreuil, 62170 Montreuil, ⊘ 21 06 07 22 (*expensive–moderate*), is a cosy inn with 4 bedrooms and serving reliably good food.

Château de Montreuil, Montreuil (*see above*).

Hotel Lancaster, Paris (*see* pp.69–74).

Connect With

Gravetye Manor, West Sussex, England (*see* pp.47–52).

Checklist

when to go

Although promoted as a year-round destination, Le Touquet is best visited in the **summer**. Its rather exposed coastal position suffers from strong winds throughout the year; these, though a welcome feature for the enthusiastic kite-flyers who frequent the beach, can prove bothersome for sunbathers. Le Touquet is popular with Parisians who use the resort as a weekend retreat. During high season, it is therefore a good idea to book well in advance.

getting there

By air: Le Touquet has its own tiny airport on the edge of the town. Transfers are available for guests staying at the Westminster Hotel. Love Air, ☏ (01279) 681435, flies daily from Biggin Hill in Kent, leaving at a civilised 9am weekdays and weekends, with an additional 6pm departure on Fridays. Love Air/Le Touquet inclusive breaks run from April through to October, linking flights with accommodation at major hotels within Le Touquet, as well as at the Château de Montreuil. Further information is available from the Le Touquet Convention & Visitors' Bureau, 375 Upper Richmond Road West, London SW14 7NX, ☏ (0181) 878 2588.

By rail: From London, take the train from Victoria to Bromley South, then a taxi to Biggin Hill. Alternatively, travel Eurostar to Calais, from where the hotel is an approximately 45-minute drive.

By road: Le Touquet is 2½ hours' drive from Paris, on Motorway 16. You could also take Le Shuttle to Calais with your car (*see* above).

entry formalities

US and Canadian citizens need full passports; British Visitor's Passports are valid.

getting by

The currency is the **French franc**. Travellers' cheques and major credit cards are accepted.

getting married

Visitors of any denomination may marry in the Catholic church of Jeanne d'Arc in Le Touquet.

Villa Argentikon Chios

Greek Islands

Villa Argentikon
82100 Chios, Greece
✆ (30 271) 31599
✉ (30 271) 31465
expensive–moderate

Tsitouras Collection
Fira, Santorini, Greece
✆ (01) 3622 326
✉ (01) 3636 738
expensive

Greek Islands: Chios

Chios is Greece's fifth-largest island, yet it has managed to escape the negative effects of mass tourism. Peaceful and unspoilt, it still has plenty to see and do. The land is largely wild and dramatically rugged, criss-crossed with pine forests, fig and olive groves; the coastline is indented with secluded pebble beaches giving on to clear, emerald-hued waters; the interior is dotted with numerous medieval fortified villages. Chios town is a lively port with friendly seafront tavernas, shops, old-fashioned bars and interesting museums. And because the island lies just 8 miles off the coast of Turkey, it is also ideally placed for day trips to Ephesus and Turkey's coastal resorts.

Villa Argentikon

The Villa Argentikon is a quite remarkable oasis, standing in the fertile plain of Campos that lies towards the south of the island. The contrast between the rather arid mountainous landscape and this lush patch of Chios is dramatic indeed—with the Argentikon providing the most vivid contrast of all. Banks of brilliant purple bougainvillaea cascade over a red and yellow sandstone wall that, fortress-like, encircles the villa; a dazzling flash of colour in what is otherwise a dusty narrow lane leading up from Chios town. Inside are magical gardens tracing a kaleidoscopic route of flowers, hedges and shrubs between just 6 suites. These are housed in 4 spacious villas, the oldest of which dates back to the 16th century.

The Villa Argentikon is owned and run by Marchese Lorenzo Argenti, who is Italian ambassador to the island and whose ancestors were among several powerful Genoese families who have lived here since the 14th century. The Italian influence is evident: once through the imposing studded bronze entrance doors, you come across an enormous, carved, swimming pool-sized marble fountain, sadly now dry but surrounded by elegant Ionic columns supporting an open vine trellis. The architecture of the individual villas also has a strong Renaissance feel. There are terracotta urns spilling geraniums, arched arbours of vines, bougainvillaea and clematis; old wells, now defunct but embellished prettily with plumbago, and a miniature orange grove, its neat trees laid out with chessboard precision.

The property has a strangely surreal aspect, akin to scenes in *Alice in Wonderland*, where the unexpected is normal and nothing is quite what it seems. Long pathways inlaid with grey and white pebbles arranged in patterns lead past marble statues of Argenti relatives massacred during the Turkish invasion of 1822. Carved dragons look out from a hidden and sheltered roof terrace. An ornamental marble pool filled with mossy green water and covered with waxy waterlilies attracts swooping dragonflies and is a cool shelter for one of the Argentikon's delightfully friendly cats.

Try to retrace your steps and the pathway seems subtly to alter, the course becoming unfathomably labyrinthine. Those banks of sweet-smelling jasmine and plumbago give way to tall clipped hedges, lit in the evening by old-fashioned wrought-iron street lamps, and you thought would be the ornamental pool is transformed into a shady alcove. Here, stone plinths are covered with comfortable cream cushions, and a large calico umbrella fights off the heat of the day.

Private Comfort

Here, the Lewis Carroll-style visual confusion increases still further: the **suites'** roof terraces overlook a carpet of green and purple foliage, out of which rise the top storeys of Argentikon's villas, set at the northern, southern, and eastern extremities of the gardens. Sitting out on the vast open-air upper floor, visitors look down on to the tree tops and hedges as if they were the ground, with the pathways, ponds and orange groves below now hidden from view so that they feel they have grown extra-tall after a sip from Alice's 'drink me' bottle.

Inside, the suites are **furnished** with truly beautiful antique *objets d'art* and furniture from the Argenti collection. Decorative walnut inlaid boxes share table-space with silver pill-boxes; beds are old-fashioned brass or wrought iron—and each suite has a living room, a kitchen area with minibar, and a large marble bathroom.

Eating In

The ethos of Argentikon is to ensure that people feel like friends of the family rather than anonymous hotel guests—indeed, the very word 'hotel' is greeted with a shudder by Lorenzo Argenti. This idea is followed through in the dining and entertaining. Breakfast is taken *en famille* in the shade of lime trees on the open-air terrace. In the evening, guests meet for cocktails and canapés, and have the choice between dining by candlelight in the open together or more privately in pairs. There is no choice to the 5-course menu, and the food is light, generally delicious; a mix of **Italian and Greek** influences is reflected in both food and wine, with the emphasis on home cooking. No lunch is provided, though Lorenzo or his assistant, Francesco, will happily suggest a good local taverna.

What to See and Do

In Chios town, the **Philip Argenti Museum**, 2 Korai Str. (*open Mon–Sat, 8–2pm*), houses an interesting collection of Argenti memorabilia including ancestral portraits of the family. In an adjacent room, the **Folklore Museum** displays antique clothing, lace, embroidery and carved woodwork from northern villages.

The island's 'resort' area is located at **Karfas Beach**, just north of Agia Fotia. A curved bay of white sand decked with umbrellas and *chaises-longues,* the sea dotted with pedalos, Karfas has good views across to the Turkish coast.

Some of the best beaches and villages are found in the **south** of the island, although there is a charming local beach with tavernas and cafés at **Agia Fotia**, 10 minutes' drive southeast from the Villa Argentikon, along the Argenti Road.

Mavra Volia, some 30 minutes' drive south from the villa, is a very popular beach with black pebbles and crystal-clear waters. Six kilometres inland from here brings you to **Pirgi**, one of the most distinctive-looking of the medieval villages. Narrow roads flanked by tall balconied houses bring the visitor to the main square, where it is easier to view the unusual decorative façades that characterize all the buildings of Pirgi. By etching away at the whitewash, the locals have created a vivid black and white patterning of flowers, birds, animals and geometric shapes. The tiny fresco-covered 13th-century church of St Apostolos (*open daily, 10–1pm*) is also worth a visit. It is located off the pretty tree-lined square, which has some friendly tavernas, ideal for a lunchtime snack.

Mesta, 15 minutes' drive west from Pirgi, is an imposing medieval walled village, its centre a web of cobbled alleys and arched lanes where houses huddle together in the shade. The main square with its snack bars and tavernas attracts tourists, but remains relatively unspoilt, with as many locals gossiping under the trees as there are backpackers.

The **west coast** has wide, empty beaches at Ornos Elatas and Irini, and cutting inland at Elinda brings the visitor to the eerily abandoned hilltop villages of Avgonima and Anavatos. On the road back to Chios, and set in a lush valley covered in pines and surrounded by tall cypress trees, is the 11th-century monastery of **Nea Moni**. The interior of its church is decorated with exquisite Byzantine mosaics.

The **north** of the island mixes arid mountainous ranges with pretty fishing villages. **Langada**, 20km north of Chios town, is a picturesque port with a good range of affordable snack bars and tavernas. **Nagos**, 30km north, with its whitewashed houses and holiday villas with their characteristic red-tiled roofs, has a small sheltered beach. There are daily ferries from Chios to Nagos.

The Villa Argentikon can arrange day trips to **Ephesus** in Turkey, and boat charters for shopping trips with lunch on the Turkish coast, or around the island.

Eating Out

Bel Air Restaurant, 118 Aegean Avenue, Chios, © 29947 (*moderate*), is a harbourside restaurant offering *mezedes* and excellent fresh fish.

El Coral Restaurant, Limenas Meston, © 76389, (*moderate–inexpensive*) offers superb salads and fresh fish in a waterside setting.

Passas Seafood Snack Bar, Langada, © 74218 (*inexpensive*). Passas specializes in traditional Greek *mezedes*.

Hotels Nearby

Villa la Favorita, Campos, Chios, © 32265 (*inexpensive*). This traditional villa offers delightful antique-filled rooms in a pretty garden setting.

Greek Islands: Santorini

Rising a dramatic 1000 feet out of an intense blue sea, and with a bleached, crystalline town clinging precariously to its craggy summit like a crust of ice on a snowy alpine range, Santorini is a most unusual-looking Greek island. In Plato's myth, Santorini appears as Atlantis, a large island with warlike inhabitants who are defeated by Athens and then destroyed in a tidal wave. Archaeological evidence shows that the island was an important Minoan settlement, shattered by a massive volcanic eruption around 1450 BC. The resulting tidal wave destroyed much of the Minoan civilization of Crete, and gave present-day Santorini its distinctive silhouette of bizarrely striated and unfathomably steep reddish-black cliffs.

The sky-high towns of Fira and Oia, with their vertigo-inducing views down to the sea-filled crater, enjoy unbeatably romantic sunsets each evening. There are some first-rate hotels and restaurants throughout the island and a lively nightlife, as well as plenty of opportunities to escape the crowds.

Tsitouras Collection

The Tsitouras Collection is the most stylish place to stay in Santorini: a meticulously restored 19th-century mansion, perched on the edge of a 1000-foot cliff in Fira. The mansion is a collection in the sense that it has been converted into 5 separate 'houses', the end result being a cluster of villas arranged around sheltered courtyards and spacious roof terraces. These whitewashed buildings, organic in shape with curved arches, twisting staircases and sloping walls, are vividly set against the backdrop of sky, sea and distant islands. On the roof terrace, a bronze bust of Maria Callas rests on a whitewashed plinth, her strong profile etched against the soft shape of a distant island. Open gateways and internal doors frame the sea below and cloud-free sky above; with no noise except the cry of a distant gull, the atmosphere is calm and dreamlike.

Private Comfort

Each house is entirely individual, and the theme of each is enhanced by appropriate antiques, paintings, and *objets d'art*.

The largest of the houses, with soaring barrel-vaulted ceilings, are the 'House of Portraits' and the 'House of Winds'. Both have 2 double bedrooms and bathrooms, and paintings and prints reflecting their evocative names. In the 'House of the Sea', the decoration centres around a pretty assortment of marine artefacts, from old shipping trunks to shells and fish sculptures, and there is fine mahogany furniture from the 18th century.

Elegantly displayed blue and white 19th-century china perfectly complements the pale lemon-coloured walls of the 'House of Porcelain' and Venetian mirrors hang alongside prints and watercolours.

For honeymooners, probably the most intimate and romantic conversion is the 'House of Nureyev', reached by a small stairway that leads to a wide terrace, half covered by a blue awning supported by columns. The house has one double bedroom, drawing room, bathroom and a raised verandah.

Public Relaxation

The Tsitouras Collection appeals to those who enjoy privacy, pampering and staying in beautiful surroundings. Typical fellow guests will include artists and writers, film stars seeking anonymity, and other honeymooners. You are generally left to your own devices, but there are opportunities to socialize.

Eating In

Breakfasts can be taken on the communal terrace, and guests occasionally get together for drinks and canapés in the evening. Dinner, for around £20 a head including wine, can be brought to guests' houses from a neighbouring restaurant, but most prefer to dine in Fira or Oia.

What to See and Do

Santorini is a smallish island, 18km by 6km at its widest. Fira itself is a pretty little town, with characteristic Cycladic architecture of white sugar-cube houses and tiny turquoise-domed whitewashed churches. It attracts hordes of tourists in high season, but you can cut through to the cliff path near the Atlantis Hotel to escape the crowds and enjoy a stunning view of the **caldera** or volcanic crater below, whose dark blue waters are a staggering 1300 feet deep.

As a volcanic island, Santorini is not renowned for its **beaches**. The sand is black and pebbly, though the eastern side of the island slopes gently down to the sea and ends in a number of large beaches, where **watersports** are plentiful. The best are at Kamari, a tourist village some 8km from Fira, and Perissa, 15km from town. There are frequent bus connections from the terminal at Theotokopoulou Square in Fira, every 15 minutes in summer months, to the 2 resorts.

It is rewarding to walk the length of **Fira**—along cobbled streets and lanes, up and down numerous steps, some of which are carved precariously near the edge of the cliff-face, towards the main shopping street filled with jewellers, goldsmiths, clothes stores and art galleries. At dusk everyone gathers to watch the sunset, and quite the most comfortable venue for this island ritual is Franco's Bar, ✆ (0286) 22881, with its terraced platforms filled with tables and chairs, all facing out to sea. Opera and classical music blasts into the darkening sky as you sip the house special, a heady champagne cocktail called a Callas. The spectacle of the changing colours of the sky, from ruby-red to glowering purple, dramatically enhanced by the music, is unforgettable. And, though the streets are full of sunset-watchers, nobody disturbs the moment, nobody speaks.

Oia, the second largest town, stands on the northernmost tip of the island, about 10km from Fira. Around the start of the century, it was Santorini's most prosperous trade and fishing village, and it still possesses some fine sea captains' houses and old wineries. Though they look somewhat similar, the atmosphere is slower, less touristy and more traditionally Greek than at Fira. Oia looks back on the curved 'crater' of Santorini and the views are particularly spectacular in the evening, when the lights of the island illuminate its serpentine silhouette like glowing pendants of topaz in a velvety dark sky. There are some fine restaurants and bars where you can sit and watch the light change.

There are a number of attractive villages on Santorini and one of the most charming is **Megalohori**, which lies in the southernmost part of the island, about 9km from Fira. Vineyards cover much of the land surrounding the village, and the church of Agios Nikolaos Marmartis at the summit, with fondant-coloured dome, fine bell tower and cool marble walls, is particularly impressive. Myriad labyrinthine lanes lead from here to villagers' homes, simple stores and a peaceful taverna sheltering under trees in the main square. The villagers are friendly and clearly animal-lovers. At the tiny supermarket next to the Vedema Hotel, the owner's cat sits on a sun-chair, resplendent with a pearl choker around its neck.

Southwest of Megalohori is the rewarding ancient site of **Akrotiri**. The archaeological excavations which took place during the sixties, uncovered a miniature Minoan Pompeii: the ancient volcanic dust had managed to preserve virtually intact village houses, frescoes, pottery, and even remnants of food from the 16th century BC.

Eating Out

Bar-Restaurant 1800, Oia, ✆ (0286) 71485 (*expensive–moderate*), is renowned for its good food and magical atmosphere.

Koukoumavalos, Oia (*moderate*), serves **French**-accented food such as stuffed crêpes, with seating outside giving spellbinding views across to Fira and Megalohori.

Hotels Nearby

Hotel Vedema, Megalohori, Santorini 84700, ✆ (0286) 81796. There are stylish apartments of varying sizes available in this high-class neoclassical hotel complex. The restaurant, a converted early 18th-century winery, serves beautifully cooked food based on local ingredients, including sea bream and scallops, plus delicious light pastries.

Checklist

when to go

The two islands have hot, dry summers, though the *meltemi* blows cooling and sometimes quite strong breezes during these months. **May, June** and **September** are probably the best months to go; throughout July and August, temperatures can climb well into the nineties, but nights can be muggy. The Villa Argentikon is most expensive in high season (17 July–3 Sept).

getting there

By air: From the UK, Excalibur fly direct to **Santorini** from Heathrow, otherwise there are direct flights to Athens with Olympic Airways, British Airways, Virgin Atlantic, British Midland and other British carriers.

From the USA, Olympic Airways flies daily to Athens (up to 9 times a week in peak periods) from New York and Boston airports. Change at Athens for the internal flight to Santorini, which takes approximately 40 minutes. The Tsitouras Collection will arrange free transfers from the airport.

Olympic Airways fly daily from Athens to **Chios**, flight time 30mins.

By sea: Ferries to **Santorini** from Piraeus and neighbouring islands are frequent. During the summer, the connections are 2–3 times a day from Piraeus, Naxos, Ios and Paros, and daily from Mykonos, and Herakleion, Crete.

At Fira, the ascent up the cliffs is made by cable car or by the traditional means: astride a donkey. Visitors with cars are able to disembark at the port of Athinios, 8km south of Fira.

Chios connects daily with Piraeus, journey time 8–10 hours.

tour operators

From the UK, packages to **Chios** including flights are available from Greek Islands Club, 66 High Street, Walton-on-Thames, Surrey KT12 1BU, ✆ (01932) 220477.

From the USA, packages to **Chios** including flights can be arranged through Twelve Islands and Beyond, 5431 MacArthur Blvd NW, Washington DC, 20016, ✆ (202) 537 3550, or toll-free ✆ (800) 345 8236, ✉ (202) 537 3548. All rates include breakfast and airport transfers.

Argo Holidays, 100 Wigmore Street, London W1H 9DR, ✆ (0171) 331 7070, and Best of Greece, 5th Floor, 23–24 Margaret Street, London W1N 8LE, ✆ (0171) 255 2320, offer reasonable packages to **Santorini** from the UK.

booking direct

To book the Tsitouras Collection, contact the head office in Athens, 80 Solonos Street, GR 10680, ✆ (01) 3622 326, ✉ (01) 3636 738.

entry formalities

US and Canadian citizens need full passports; a British Visitor's Passport is valid for stays of up to 3 months.

health

Immunization against hepatitis A is recommended. Take mosquito repellent.

getting around

On **Chios**, a car is essential and car hire is inexpensive. The Villa Argentikon will organise car hire for guests. On **Santorini**, taxis are relatively cheap, or you can hire a **car** from Santostar Travel in Fira, ✆ (0286) 23105, 23227, 23082. They will also arrange organised tours of the islands, as well as day- and half-day cruises to neighbouring islands.

getting by

Although **Greek** is useful, **English** and **German** are widely spoken. The currency is the **Greek drachma**. Major credit cards are accepted on Chios and Santorini, though the Villa Argentikon will only take cash or personal cheques.

Ireland: County Clare

Dromoland Castle
Newmarket-on-Fergus, Co. Clare, Ireland
✆ (353 61) 368144
✉ (353 61) 363355
expensive–moderate

Nothing quite prepares the visitor for the intense green of Ireland's landscape: lushly verdant lanes fringed with feathery hedgerows, the patchwork of fields tinged with different hues, the long grass covering gentle hills that run down to a dramatic black rocky coastline. In many ways, the countryside seems almost entirely untouched by the 20th century.

Each of Ireland's 32 counties has a highly individual character, but for honeymooners seeking a relaxing retreat in the country, with access to fine deserted beaches, friendly villages, good restaurants and pubs, the counties of Clare and Kerry in the west and southwest probably provide the best bases for touring.

For a taste of true Irish eccentricity, summer visitors should head for County Kerry's annual three-day Puck Fair, staged in mid-August at Killorgin. Recalling old fertility rites, the locals crown a large billy goat as king and garland the beast with flowers. At the end of the month, the famous 'Rose of Tralee' competition selects its favourite Irish female from hordes of competitors from all over the world. In September there is the Galway Oyster Festival and (though hopefully this is of merely academic interest to honeymooners) the Matchmaking Festival in Lisdoonvarna, County Clare, during which optimistic bachelor farmers gather to find their ideal woman.

Dromoland Castle

Dromoland Castle is an exceptionally friendly and romantic hotel, situated just 8 miles north of Shannon airport. Built for the O'Brien clan, who are direct descendants of 'Brian Boru', the High King of Ireland, this handsome turreted stone castle with its lakeside setting dates back to the 16th century.

Arrive late on a summer's evening and the castle looks at its most magical. The sky, still light, casts a blue-grey phosphorescent softness over the stone façades, a rich golden glow emanates from the large mullioned windows on both the ground and first floors and the air is quiet, save for the odd voice or the rustle of a wood pigeon in the nearby parkland. The delightfully unstuffy staff are attentive and welcoming. Guests' gastronomic needs are deemed to be of immediate importance; checking-in procedures can wait. And should you arrive too late for dinner and request a sandwich or snack, you are likely receive an enormous and delicious platter of wild smoked salmon, oysters and Irish soda bread, served up with the homely explanation that: 'You might just feel a bit peckish later on'. Footmen, porters and waiters seem able to turn their hands to the most bizarre of requests—including, recently, removing a large moth from the bedroom of a phobic guest and providing stale bread in the morning for feeding to the family of Dromoland ducks parading beneath the ground-floor windows.

Private Comfort

Bedrooms are enormous, comfortable and old-fashioned; most enjoy views of the wooded parklands and the lake. **Furnishings** are in the style of a grand family home, with pretty floral prints, padded window-seats, delicate pinstriped wallpaper, and plenty of magazines, guidebooks and novels provided.

Public Relaxation

Ancestral portraits of dour-faced O'Briens, heavy antiques, stone carvings and dark, richly coloured fabrics characterize the furnishings in the public rooms yet, despite its imposing surroundings, Dromoland is a genuinely relaxing place to stay. Offsetting the grandeur are comfortable, rather unglamorous chairs and sofas ranged along the length of the **main gallery** and, in the evening, log fires are lit to add an atmosphere of warmth to the surroundings as much as to raise the temperature.

Dromoland's large estate incorporates facilities for golf, tennis, cycling, jogging, fishing and boating. Horse riding, flying lessons, helicopter tours (great for aerial views of the thrashing waves washing the steep Cliffs of Moher) and deep-sea fishing can be arranged locally. And, for the less actively inclined, there are romantic walled gardens filled with roses for lazy afternoons.

Eating In

The cooking at Dromoland is of a high standard, with much use of **Irish produce**. Breakfasts are belt-busting affairs, incorporating local bacon, kidneys, black pudding and eggs. In the evening, the somewhat austerely furnished main dining-room serves house specialities including fillet of lamb served with *foie gras*, and steamed turbot with braised fennel. Ask to visit the large, well-stocked wine cellar.

What to See and Do

Approximately 10 miles east of Dromoland are 2 interesting 15th- and 16th-century castles: **Bunratty** (*open daily from 9.30am*), with its 3 'murder holes' that allowed its inhabitants to pour boiling oil

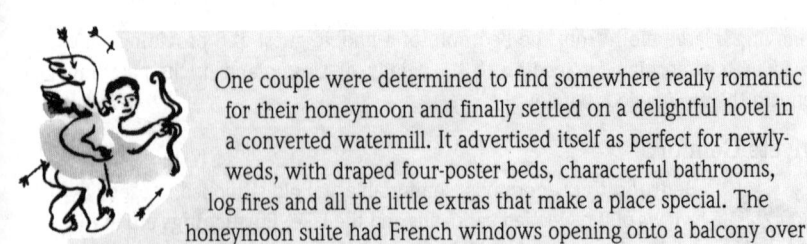

One couple were determined to find somewhere really romantic for their honeymoon and finally settled on a delightful hotel in a converted watermill. It advertised itself as perfect for newly-weds, with draped four-poster beds, characterful bathrooms, log fires and all the little extras that make a place special. The honeymoon suite had French windows opening onto a balcony over a picturesque millpond covered in waterlilies. 'When we arrived I was overwhelmed,' remembers the bride. 'It was stunningly beautiful and just like the brochure.' Unfortunately the brochure had omitted one major detail—mosquitoes. 'When we got up to the room after dinner it was full of them. We spent what should have been the most romantic night of our lives swatting—and the next 10 days scratching...'

on to their attackers below, and **Craggaunowen** (*open daily, March–October; 10–6pm*), famed for its ringed fort. While at Bunratty, stop for a Guinness at the famous olde worlde pub, Durty Nelly's (✆ *(061) 364072*).

Limerick, Ireland's third largest city, lies 20 miles east of Dromoland. The old part of town around St Mary's Cathedral has fine Georgian town houses, and, in Castle Street, the recently restored King John's Castle (*open daily, 9.30-5pm, April–Sept*), orginally built by the Normans, provides good views from its towers over the Shannon and the town.

Dingle Bay (approximately 80 miles southwest of the hotel) is set in a glorious part of the Kerry coastline and, despite the crowds who gather here in hope of sighting Fungie the Dolphin, it is worth allocating a day for visiting both the bay and the peninsula. The landscape is unspoilt and rugged, fringed with long, sandy beaches, sheltered by steep cliffs. Dingle is the chief town of the peninsula—a small fishing community which swells to double its size in the summer months. There are good crafts shops, restaurants and pubs, and, a must for dolphin-spotters, boat trips leave hourly (£5).

Eating Out

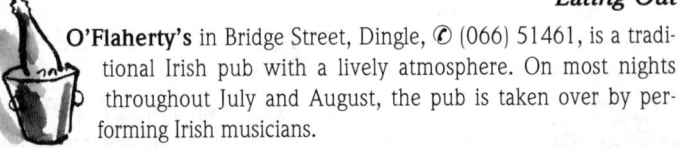

O'Flaherty's in Bridge Street, Dingle, ✆ (066) 51461, is a traditional Irish pub with a lively atmosphere. On most nights throughout July and August, the pub is taken over by performing Irish musicians.

Doyle's Seafood Bar, John Street, Dingle, ✆ (066) 51174 (*moderate*), is great for fresh, simply cooked seafood served in unpretentious surroundings.

Hotels Nearby

★★★★★**Ashford Castle**, Cong, Co. Mayo, ✆ (9092) 46003. The sister castle to Dromoland, this luxury hotel dates back to the 13th century.

★★★★**Kilkea Castle**, Castledermot, Co. Kildare, ✆ (350) 3345156, is an austere but comfortable hotel with an impressive Great Hall and honeymoon suites in circular turrets.

Checklist

when to go

Summer is the most popular time to visit Ireland: the weather is pleasant, if unpredictable, temperatures rarely climbing higher than 20°C. The countryside is also at its most lush and green at this time.

getting there

By air: From the UK, Aer Lingus and Ryanair fly direct to Shannon airport from most major cities. From the USA, Aer Lingus fly to Shannon Airport from New York and Boston. Delta flies direct from Atlanta.

By ferry/road: From the UK, the 2 points of entry are Cork City and Rosslare in Co. Wexford. Allow 3–4 hours for driving cross-country to Dromoland.

tour operators

From the UK, fly–drive and ferry packages to Dromoland Castle can be booked through **Crystal Premier Britain**, Crystal House, The Courtyard, Arlington Road, Surbiton, Surrey KT6 6BW, ✆ (0181) 390 8513 and **Aer Lingus**, ✆ (0181) 899 4747. From the USA, reservations can be made through **Celtic International Tours**, 161 Central Avenue, Albany, NY 11206, toll-free ✆ (800) 833 4373 and **Destination Ireland**, 250 W 57th Street, Suite 2511, New York, NY 10107, ✆ (212) 977 9629.

booking direct

Reservations can be made from USA, toll-free ✆ (800) 346 7007 or through the **Relais & Châteaux** New York Sales Office, ✆ (212) 8560115.

entry formalities

US and Canadian citizens need full passports; UK citizens need no passports but should carry some identification.

getting around

A **car** is essential. The major rentalcompanies are represented at Shannon airport.

getting by

The currency is the **Irish pound** or **punt**. Major credit cards are accepted.

getting married

Marriages can be performed here.

Italy: Florence

Villa San Michele
Via Doccia 4, 50014 Fiesole, Florence, Italy
✆ (39 55) 59451/2
✉ (39 55) 598734
expensive

Tuscany offers all that is seductively Italian: some of the most glorious art and architecture, and one of the best combinations of climate, countryside and cuisine in Europe. There are gloriously handsome medieval hilltop towns with turreted castles serrating the skyline and wonderful historic cities, notably Florence, where a thriving contemporary culture co-exists with the rich art treasures of the Renaissance. The countryside is delightfully varied, from the fertile valleys, vineyards and gentle pine-studded hills of 'Chiantishire' to the wild mountains on the Umbrian border. Tuscan food embraces the best of Italian cooking, being characterized by strong flavours and healthy, fresh, local ingredients.

A touring honeymoon through Tuscany, based in Fiesole, a pretty suburb of Florence, offers a satisfying mix of city sightseeing and day trips to such beautiful towns as Siena, Arezzo and Cortona. Leisurely days can be spent shopping in Florence or picnicking near olive groves with a bottle of local wine, some strong pecorino cheese and fresh juicy figs and later dining in a romantic hillside taverna.

Villa San Michele

Villa San Michele is one of Europe's most romantic hideaways, a hotel renowned for the beauty of its architecture and its stunning setting. This luxurious retreat was formerly a Franciscan monastery, thought to be designed by Michelangelo, and now it is classed among the Italian National Trust monuments.

It is located a 15-minute drive from the centre of Florence, past the train station and the large holiday villas of wealthy Italians, then upwards at Fiesole to the villa's own terraced hillside. Shielded by regal conifers and soaring cypresses, the hotel appears on the horizon, its graceful cream- and grey-stone arcaded façade testifying to its pure Renaissance pedigree.

Private Comfort

Upstairs, heavy wooden doors with faded Roman numerals mark the bedrooms. Carved antique wedding chests line the corridor. A bowl of green leaves decorated with an exceedingly large ruby-red apple, polished to waxy perfection, adds a splash of colour.

There are only 28 **bedrooms** and **suites**, all fashioned from the cells once used by Franciscan monks, and though they are luxuriously equipped, the feeling of calm and simplicity still pervades. The most modest 'cells' feature wrought-iron beds canopied with cream calico, Turkey rugs, wooden chests, armoires, desks and pretty leaded-light windows framed by shutters. The views are breathtaking panoramas stretching down the valley and across to Florence, with Brunelleschi's distinctive dome silhouetted against the mist.

The best views of Florence are from rooms 3 to 7, but room 1, which overlooks the terraced garden and boasts its own wrought-iron deck chairs, is also exceedingly charming. For sheer luxury, the **Michelangelo Suite** is pretty impressive. There is a massive stone fireplace opposite which the king-size bed is set on a raised pedestal. The bathroom, with its huge mahogany jacuzzi bath, has comfortable thick-pile bathrobes and generous supplies of soaps, bath salts and gels, all exquisitely packaged in marbled-paper boxes and gold-stoppered bottles.

There are modern '**junior suites**' in the gardens with faxes and televisions. The **Limonia Suite**, so named after the lemon grove that once grew there, is set apart from the hotel and is a popular retreat for honeymooners. But half the fun of staying at the villa is to experience a night or two in a luxuriously kitted out monastic cell, with no television and only a telephone to testify to the 20th century.

Public Relaxation

All hotel trappings everywhere, from reception desk to bar, are eclipsed by well-placed and sturdy antique furnishings. And, in keeping with its original purpose, there is no room for flashy effects at the Villa San Michele. The purity of the architecture is allowed to dominate, and simplicity is a keynote in all furnishings. Floors throughout are either wooden or brick and covered with rugs. A fine triptych fresco of the *Last Supper*, though not perhaps an ideal backdrop for a hotel **bar**, serves to set the terracotta and sage colour scheme and tempers the modern effect of sofas and chairs. The hotel has an outdoor **swimming pool** in the **gardens**, and provides regular shuttle services daily into the centre of Florence.

Eating In

In summer months, guests dine on the flower-filled, vaulted open loggia, with its views over Monte Albano to the west, the Chianti hills to the south and Florence, pierced through by the River Arno, in the valley below. When the sun is at its hottest, cream calico blinds are let down to shield the diners; in the evening each table is romantically candlelit. The cooking is unforgettable—the simpler the dish, the more memorable it seems to be. Delicate tortelloni stuffed with aubergine and served with a cheese sauce really does melt in the mouth, and an plain grilled sea bass served with spinach and a salad is delicious.

What to See and Do

There is much to see and do in this superb city; if time is limited, head straight for the **Piazza del Duomo** and visit the cathedral and the baptistry (both *open daily*), the oldest building in Florence. The gilded doors of the baptistry clearly illustrate the stylistic development from Andrea Pisano's expressively Gothic figures to Lorenzo Ghiberti's Renaissance purity and invention.

The **Accademia**, Via Ricasoli 60 (*open Tues–Sat 9–2pm; Sun 9–1pm; closed Mon*), is where Michelangelo's famous gargantuan statue of David resides. Further Renaissance treasures can be found in rooms 7–15 of the **Uffizi**, Piazzale degli Uffizi 6 (*open Tues–Sat, 9–7pm; Sun, 9–1pm; closed Mon*). Limit yourselves to these rooms first, since this gallery houses nearly 2000 works of art and trying to cover all the exhibits is a daunting task.

Cross the Arno via the picturesque if touristy **Ponte Vecchio**. The present bridge dates from 1345 and, as it was in medieval Florence, it is still a Mecca for jewellers and their clients.

The **Boboli Gardens** located just south of the river are among the most lovely of Italian pleasure gardens. A great refuge from the heat of the day, they are rich in visual Mannerist jokes, fine statuary, fountains, plants and pools. Standing on the highest of the hills southeast of the city is the 11th-century **San Miniato**. The oldest and perhaps prettiest church in Florence, its distinctive façade of green, white and black marble can be seen from all over the city.

Siena, 68km south of Florence, distinctive with its warm brown brick buildings, its medieval towers and palaces and its soaring skyline, is the setting for the famous Palio, the bareback horse race that takes place around the town's lovely Campo on July 2nd and 16th. It is an enormously important event in Siena and consequently heavily attended; the rehearsals on the days running up to the Palio are less crowded, just as interesting, and can be viewed in comfort from one of the restaurants lining the Campo. The black and white Gothic cathedral is glorious.

Arezzo, 81km southeast of Florence, is an attractive hill town with a lovely 14th-century cathedral, a lively main square with a handsome loggia designed by Vasari, and, in the Franciscan basilica of San Francesco, fine frescoes depicting the *Legend of the True Cross* painted by Piero della Francesca. An enormous antiques market is held in Piazza Grande on the first Sunday of every month.

The relatively tourist-free hilltop town of **Cortona**, 102km southeast of Florence, is quintessentially Tuscan, its mellow sandstone buildings wrapped in medieval walls. A Saturday market is staged in the Piazza Garibaldi and, from mid-August to mid-September, Cortona hosts an annual antiques fair.

Eating Out

Osteria le Logge, off the Campo, at Via del Porrione 33, Siena, ✆ (0577) 48013 (*moderate; closed Sun*), offers superb pastas, great risottos and guinea-fowl.

Il Tirabuscio, Via dei Benci 34, Florence, ✆ (055) 247622 (*moderate–inexpensive*), has a charming atmosphere and serves local specialities and excellent puddings.

Hotels Nearby

***Hotel Santa Caterina**, Via Piccolomini 7, Siena, ✆ (0577) 221105 (*moderate–inexpensive*), is a converted 18th-century villa with attractively decorated rooms.

Connect With

*****Hotel Splendido**, Portofino (*see* pp.103–108).

Checklist

when to go

May and September are excellent months for touring Tuscany. The weather is still warm, though the temperatures have dropped low enough to make sightseeing a comfortable experience. Ideally, Florence should be avoided from June to August when the narrow streets become congested with tourists, and museums are impossibly full. If you have to take your honeymoon in these months, make sure to book a hotel well in advance of travel. The Villa San Michele is closed from mid-November to mid-March.

getting there

By air: From the UK, the most convenient airport for Tuscany is Pisa. British Airways, Alitalia and Air UK have direct flights from London to Pisa. From the US, the major carriers are Air Canada and TWA to Rome, or you can fly to the UK and transfer on.

By rail: Pisa's Galileo airport and Rome's Fiumicino airport are connected by a regular train service to Florence's Santa Maria Novella station. Transfers to the Villa San Michele are available.

tour operators

In the UK, **Magic of Italy** and **Italian Escapades**, both at 227 Shepherds Bush Road, London W6 7AS, ✆ (0181) 748 7575, will tailor-make honeymoons in Tuscany, including accommodation at the Villa San Michele. A honeymoon programme is available.

booking direct

From the USA, the Villa San Michele can be booked through **The Leading Hotels of the World**, toll-free ✆ (800) 223 6800; or through **Orient-Express Hotels**, toll-free ✆ (800) 237 1236; or through the **Relais & Châteaux** New York Sales Office, ✆ (212) 856 0115.

entry formalities

US and Canadian citizens need full passports; a British Visitor's Passport is valid for stays of up to 3 months.

getting around

Car hire is recommended for touring Tuscany, though it is not necessary for exploring Florence. The major rental companies are represented at Pisa and Rome airports.

getting by

The currency is the **Italian lira**. Major credit cards are accepted.

getting married

Marriages can be performed here.

Italy: Portofino

Hotel Splendido
Viale Baratta 13, 16035 Portofino, Italy
✆ (39 185) 26 95 51
✇ (39 185) 26 96 14
expensive

In summer, Italy can seem like one big stifling museum, as crowds of visitors attempt the modern-day equivalent of the Grand Tour. Yet the country has as much to offer in terms of peace and seclusion as it has in richly historical cities and towns. There are a number of relatively unspoilt holiday resorts, principally favoured by Italian families wishing to escape foreign visitors, that manage to avoid many of the uglier traits of tourism.

Head for Portofino on the Ligurian Riviera (approximately 2 hours' drive northwest of Florence), and you won't be disturbed by tawdry street vendors plying their 'artistic' skills in ugly charcoal caricatures. Nor will the waterfront cafés serve you orange juice in an unmanageably large Venetian glass goblet, complete with miniature gondola floating on a slice of tired-looking fruit. Here, waiters prefer that you make your own decision about entering their establishment. For Portofino has kept its profile as a quietly sophisticated seaside resort, a favourite setting for illicit trysts of the rich and famous, little changed since the late film director Federico Fellini effectively immortalised its lotus-eating charms in the 1960 film *La Dolce Vita*.

Hotel Splendido

Rex Harrison, one of Hollywood's most memorable post-war rakes, admired Portofino so much that he built a holiday home in the hills behind the harbour. Friends flocked to 'Sexy Rexy's' villa, and any surplus chums were accommodated in the luxurious Hotel Splendido across the bay.

Originally a Benedictine monastery, the Splendido was transformed into a luxury hotel in 1902, and it still retains an atmosphere of understated Edwardian grandeur. The approach to the hotel is pretty dramatic—a terrifying course of giddy hairpin bends, but you will be amply rewarded as the Splendido looms into sight. If your nerves are shattered, leave the car by the entrance for someone else to park, stretch your shaking legs and head for the grand outdoor terrace. Extending along the length of the hotel, adorned with flower-filled terracotta pots and urns and set for a delicious alfresco lunch, the terrace provides a romantic view over the town. Directly below, white yachts, colourful fishing boats and sleek gin-palaces bob together on a glinting dark jade sea, just yards from Portofino's naturally sheltered harbour. On a small pine-clad promontory to the left, one can just glimpse the ochre-toned stone silhouette of the castle. To the right, miles of lush green forested land marks the hiking trail to the charming fishing village of San Fruttuoso.

Private Comfort

All **bedrooms** overlook the bay and pine forests; even the smallest has the benefit of a sea-facing balcony, adorned with trailing geraniums and furnished with wrought-iron table and chairs for romantic breakfasts away from the other guests. The larger balconies provide plenty of room for private sunbathing on comfortably cushioned recliners.

Furnishings are kept elegantly low-key: thick-pile cream carpets and rugs, pink-painted panelled walls, the odd mural of flowers or ferns, plump sofas and grand, firmly sprung beds dressed in crisp cool linen sheets.

The huge **bathrooms** are veritable temples for the body-conscious: pale blue fluffy bathrobes, towels and wash-mitts come embellished with the hotel's logo of a seahorse; baths feature jacuzzi jets which, at full throttle, would shame the strongest of Swedish masseuses; and walk-in power showers almost pin you to the tiles in a body-slapping drench of warm water. Toothbrush and toothpaste, hand-milled soaps and expensive bath gels are provided and, for a taste of true luxury, you can use the bathroom's private telephone extension and stereo link-up with the bedroom's state-of-the-art sound system as you bathe in a froth of fragrant foam.

Public Relaxation

The public rooms are invitingly relaxing, most guests take to the **bar** in the evening for a 'Splendido', the hotel's speciality cocktail of Prosecco and wild strawberry. Covering the walls are numerous compelling black and white photographs of all the stars who have ever stayed at the hotel. In fact, it is well worth asking to see the hotel's leather-bound visitors' book; this encyclopaedia of the famous is compulsive reading, a valuable *Who's Who* of 20th-century royalty, music and film stars, writers, society figures and politicians. Madonna, it seems, was far too busy during her stay here to put pen to paper, and offered instead to take the book away with her, with a vague promise to return it 'some time', signed. I'm happy to report that the Splendido refused.

Sports and leisure facilities include a **tennis court**, decent-sized **swimming pool**, **beauty parlour** with sauna and massage, and **hairdresser**.

Eating In

Candlelit dinner is taken in the open, on the **terrace**. Pastas are superb, making full use of the brilliant green, intensely flavoured pesto sauce that is a speciality of the region. Pumpkin ravioli with rosemary, spaghetti with fresh prawns and calamari, as well as simply grilled sea bass are some other star features on this interestingly varied menu.

During the day, lunches are served at the **poolside barbecue**.

What to See and Do

The hotel provides helpful and detailed guides, enhanced with delicate watercolour illustrations, to good **walks** in the area. One of the most enjoyable of these is the gentle 2-mile stroll to the tiny fishing harbour of **San Fruttuoso**, a cove accessible only on foot or by boat. The walk takes you through a coastal conservation trail above the Splendido, on a route that has been used by locals for hundreds of years and remains exactly the same as in the past, bar a few helpful red arrow pointers to keep you on the straight and narrow. The path leads you through pine forests, past holiday villas, high above steep slopes that plunge cleanly into the Ligurian sea, and past straggling olive groves; in the autumn you can watch the tiny succulent fruits being harvested by hand. Husband-and-wife teams work side by side, the husband scaling the trees to shake the branches while the wife stands below, gathering the olives into fine nets. The walk finally spirals down to the 10th-century **abbey** of San Fruttuoso, its graceful Gothic cloisters rising as if directly out of the pebbles in this secluded and miniature inlet. The cliffs circling the bay, the small beach populated by families of sunbathing cats, the rich Mediterranean vegetation climbing the steep hill behind, the sparkling sea and above all the complete absence of noise, give San Fruttuoso a blessedly calming and relaxing atmosphere. And this feast of natural beauty soon gives way to another form of nourishment, for there are some first-rate simple beach restaurants around the bay for lunch. After your meal, you need not walk back; the regular ferry service will return you to Portofino Mare.

Portofino itself resembles a stage set for a particularly jolly Rossini opera. The harbour fronts a cobbled piazza, a natural stage upon which stroll chic European sightseers and millionaire yacht-owners. Only their Gucci loafers distinguish the latter from weather-beaten, espadrille-clad local fishermen. Moving at a faster pace are deft-limbed waiters, weaving in and out of the portside cafés and fish restaurants. Fruit and vegetable stores and pasta shops intermingle with souvenir shops—this is a place to stop, sip a cappuccino and watch the world go by.

The delights of Portofino can be sampled within an hour or so. You can climb to the castle, look round a couple of churches, admire the rust-coloured fishermen's houses curving round the quayside, and spend vast amounts of lire on a yachtie's T-shirt, but you will soon want to go a little farther afield for amusement.

The city of **Genoa**, Christopher Columbus' birthplace, is about 30 minutes' drive westwards from Portofino. An important mercantile port, it has a colourful covered market, a range of clothes shops along the Via XX Settembre and a higgledy-piggledy historical centre enclosing narrow alleys and small piazzas, in contrast to the elegant Baroque buildings of the Piazza Campetto.

Santa Margharita Ligure, the easterly neighbour of Portofino, is a lively and picturesque fishing town with some reasonably priced restaurants and busy harbour bars. An hour or so further east are 5 clifftop fishing villages known collectively as the Cinque Terre. At the last of these, **Riomaggiore**, you can walk along the famous picturesque cliffside path known as the Via dell'Amore and copy the young Italian couples who draw inspiration from its name and linger among its rocky inlets for a passionate smooch!

Lerici and **La Spezia** lie on the other side of the Portovenere promontory, where the poet Shelley drowned. Both enjoy sheltered coves which are ideal for picnics and sunbathing.

Eating Out

Delfino's, Portofino, ✆ (0039) 185 286667 (*expensive*). Facing the harbour at Portofino is this fashionable fish restaurant, a firm favourite of the stars over the years, judging by the photos of Rod Stewart, Aristotle Onassis, Maria Callas and Federico Fellini. Grilled crayfish and fresh sea bass are delicious here.

Frantoio, Santa Margherita Ligure, ✆ (0039) 185 269081 (*moderate*), a converted olive mill, serves meltingly tasty pasta, robust meat dishes and fresh fish.

At **San Fruttuoso**, any of the beachside restaurants (*cheap*), are worth trying for lunch. Feast on *trenette*, the local pasta resembling mouse-tails, and pesto, greener and more pungent in flavour than any shop-bought variety. Follow with fresh squid and scampi, washed down with local white wine.

Hotels Nearby

★★**Eden**, Vico Dritto 18, ✆ 269091 (*expensive*), is a charming 12-room hotel in town with a garden and good Ligurian restaurant.

Connect With

★★★★★**Grand-Hotel du Cap Ferrat**, St-Jean-Cap-Ferrat (*see* pp.63–68).

★★★★★**Villa San Michele**, Fiesole, Florence (*see* pp.97–102).

Checklist

when to go

Late spring and early autumn are ideal times for a stay in Portofino. All year round, the town does everything in its power to ward off too many visitors: cars are banned from the port, parking in the underground car park is prohibitively expensive; yet the narrow coastal road to the centre of the town can still become one long traffic jam during July and August, and so these high season months are best avoided.

getting there

By air: The Hotel Splendido is 30km from Genoa's Christopher Columbus International Airport, with connections to other Italian cities and major European destinations.

By rail: The hotel is 6km from Santa Margherita station, linking with Turin, Milan, Pisa and Rome.

By road: Drive via Motorway A14, taking the Rapallo exit (8 km).

tour operators

From the UK, **Italian Escapades**, 227 Shepherds Bush Road, London W6 7AS, ✆ (0181) 748 2661, organise individually tailored packages to the hotel. **Elegant Resorts**, The Old Palace, Chester CH1 1RB, ✆ (012 44) 897 777, offer week-long packages, inclusive of private car transfer.

booking direct

Through **Orient-Express Hotels** reservations: from the UK, ✆ (0181) 568 8366; from the USA, toll-free ✆ (800) 992 5055. Also **Relais & Châteaux** New York, ✆ (212) 8560115 and **Leading Hotels of the World**: UK freefone ✆ (0800) 181 123; USA toll-free ✆ (800) 223 6800.

getting around

Car hire is recommended. The hotel organises rentals with Hertz and Avis. The major rental companies are represented at Genoa Airport.

getting by

The currency is the **Italian lira**. Major credit cards are accepted. US and Canadian citizens need full passports; a British Visitor's Passport is valid for stays of up to 3 months.

getting married

Marriages can be performed here.

Italy: Portofino

Italy: Amalfi Coast

Le Sirenuse
Via Cristoforo Colombo 30, 84017 Positano, Italy
✆ (39 89) 875066
📠 (39 89) 811798
expensive–moderate

Italy's Amalfi coastline, snaking south from Naples through to Salerno, is celebrated for its beauty. A tortuous route of around 80km that swoops around steep limestone cliffs and dips down into quiet fishing villages, it offers magical views at every curve. Fragrant lemon groves, the cloudy silhouettes of umbrella pines and the hazy outline of Capri shimmering in the bay are replaced by the narrow lanes of clifftop towns. Here simple whitewashed apartment blocks huddle close, their decorative balconies spilling over with red geraniums and drying clothes flapping in the breeze. Some, like pretty Positano, are terraced into the cliff-face, their streets a zigzag of steep stone steps leading up from the sea. Others, Sorrento in particular, have majestic seaside hotels following the contour of the coastline, a testimony to their historic location on the travellers' trail. Today their trade is less discriminating, as they seek to lure coachloads of tourists with tawdry souvenirs, pizzas, chips and sentimental songs.

This is a route that, by its sheer variety, is immensely rewarding to explore, but bear in mind the journey from one end to the other can be pretty hair-raising, especially for inexperienced drivers. To cover the coastline fully requires around four or five days of sightseeing. In high season the road is chock-a-block with coaches and cars, so stick to either late spring or early autumn.

Positano is halfway along the Amalfi coastal road as it climbs up from a curved and sheltered bay. A chic and visually charming seaside town, it has houses, cafés and hotels terraced into every available space, each building perched precariously on top of the other. Even late into the season the town is adorned with purple bougainvillaea and wayward vines that knit together to form a natural roof over the narrow cobbled lanes.

From the sea, Positano resembles a vibrant stage set; colourful fishing boats and umbrellas cover the black sand beach; overhead, the villas, bars and hotels project from the cliff face like elaborate theatre boxes. This is appropriate, for at night-time the curving bay creates a singular acoustic effect: each noise—a dog barking in the distance, the plash of waves, a mournful guitar song—echoes, enlarges and mingles in harmony with the others.

Le Sirenuse

Centrally located on one of the best hillside spots is Le Sirenuse. Originally 3 neighbouring 18th-century Neapolitan homes, the buildings have been converted by the family of the Marchese Sersale, descendants of one of the original owners, into a supremely elegant 5-star family inn. All of the 60 bedrooms and suites enjoy enchanting views over the roof-tops of Positano (including the colourful tiled dome of the town's principal church) and out to the sea to the rocky outcrops of Li Galli, three islands that lie about 6 km out in the bay. The ballet star Rudolf Nureyev had his summer residence on the largest of these islands, but they were made famous first by myth and legend. Homer tells of the Sirens who lived on the Galli islands—perilous beauties whose songs were so unbearably seductive that Ulysses had to be strapped to the mast of his ship in order to resist them.

Private Comfort

Le Sirenuse's **bedrooms** are elegantly minimalist. Cool, decorative tiles and mosaics cover the floors. There are oil-paintings and antiques belonging to the Sersale family, and the enormous beds are dressed in crisp cotton monogrammed sheets. Even as you lie in bed, the sparkling sea is visible through large French windows. And the private **balconies**, adorned with terracotta urns, geraniums and ferns, each furnished with loungers, table and chairs, provide the perfect romantic venue for a breakfast with a view. There is air-conditioning, and luxurious marble **bathrooms** feature jacuzzi baths, fluffy bathrobes and expensive scented soaps and shampoos.

Public Relaxation

On the ground floor, extending the length of the hotel, is an exquisite terrace with views out to sea. Half of this is taken up by a **swimming pool** surrounded by white loungers which rival the beds for sheer comfort. At the far end is a small vine-covered **bar** set into a niche decorated with mosaics of the Sirens. The hotel's main American bar features live **music** in the evening and offers an imaginative range of cocktails. The other half of the terrace is an **open-air dining** area leading off from the dining-room itself, dotted with white enamelled filigree chairs and tables, huge stone urns filled with palms and climbing purple bougainvillaea, and punctuated by sturdy pillars covered in lush green climbers. Set between each pair of pillars are cushioned benches which offer stunning panoramas of the town and bay.

Eating In

Huge and delicious buffet **breakfasts** are taken on the terrace, and these pretty much set you up for the day. Dishes include scrambled eggs, sausages and bacon, tasty miniature *bocconicini* mozzarellas, tiny juicy tomatoes, rustic breads and warm muffins, mortadella, fresh doughnuts and steaming hot coffee. Breakfasts are included in the daily room rate, though the restaurant serves lunch and dinner as well (*expensive*). The cooking, featuring local **Neapolitan** specialities with heavy use of seafood, mozzarella, herbs and pastas, is average but worth trying for one evening meal, if only for the romantic ambience.

What to See and Do

Le Sirenuse's motor boat is available for daily excursions to **Li Galli** and beyond. Public **tennis courts** are within walking distance of the hotel, and **waterskiing** off Positano can be arranged. The hotel will also organise tailor-made sightseeing itineraries for guests. All of the following can easily be undertaken within a day:

The island of **Capri** is accessible by ferry from Positano (*daily; 18,000 lire return*). The journey past Li Galli and along the coast takes about an hour, though in high season there is a hydrofoil that cuts the journey down to 20 minutes. There are boat tours from Capri Harbour to the numerous grottoes that dot the rocky shoreline. The two principal, picturesque villages, Capri and Anacapri, make good starting points for walking tours through this lush and extremely hilly island. On the northeastern tip are the ruins of the Villa Jovis, the retirement home of the Emperor Tiberius (*open Tues–Sun, 9am to 1 hour before sunset*). The stairway behind the little church leads to Tiberius' Leap, the spot from which slaves were reputedly thrown over the cliffs and into the sea.

Pompeii, an hour's drive west from Positano along the A3 autostrada (exit at Pompeii Scavi), should not be missed. Buried under the volcanic ash of Vesuvius in AD 79, the site provides the most vivid picture of life in a Roman city at the time of the Empire. The site, ✆ 081 8621181, (*open daily, 9–6pm, except Mon and hols; 12,000 lire*) is vast and fascinating. Highlights include the splendid frescoes in the House of Mysteries, the Stabian Baths with its well-preserved swimming pools, the lavishly decorated House of the Vetii, and the brothel, complete with erotic frescoes and stone beds.

Amalfi is 40 minutes' drive east of Positano. Buses leave approximately every 30 minutes from the stop to the right of the hotel's exit (*4,800 lire; tickets must be* *bought in advance from the newsagents' opposite the hotel*). Amalfi is surrounded by steeply terraced lemon groves and has an impressive cathedral that was founded in the 9th century. It retains its orginal bell tower but much of the polychrome façade, reached by a steep flight of steps, was rebuilt in the 19th century. To the left of the *duomo* is a beautiful cloister surrounded by Arabic-style arcades. From the cathedral square, lanes lead into the old town, a labyrinth of tiny cobbled alleys and staircases, small cafés and artisan shops. From the very top of the old town is a splendid view over the bay.

Ravello enjoys a magically beautiful setting, perched like a magnificent balcony over the Gulf of Salerno. Just 20 minutes'drive inland from Amalfi on route 373, it is a hillside town of ancient towers, arches, narrow streets and fine villas. There are some first-rate restaurants and hotels, and interesting pottery shops. Wagner stayed here, at the Villa Rúfolo (*open daily; free entrance on Thurs*), and was inspired by the dreamy surroundings to write his *Parsifal*. A terrace along the edge of the villa's gardens hangs over a sheer drop that falls away to the sea below.

Eating Out

Positano has some reasonably priced trattorias at the beach's edge, with plenty of outside tables. Of these, **Tre Sorelli**, ✆ 875 452 (*moderate*), is particularly friendly and good for seafood and pizzas.

Albergo Giordano e Villa Maria, Via S Chiara 2, 84010 Ravello, ✆ (089) 857255 (*moderate*), is a charming restaurant with a magnificent terrace and fine views out to sea. Specialities include pasta, grilled sea bass and *tiramisu*. A small hotel as well, it has a small number of pretty antique-filled bedrooms.

La Savardina, Vialo Capo 8, Capri, ✆ (081) 8376300 (*moderate–inexpensive*), is an enchanting garden trattoria set beneath the Villa Jovis, run by the eccentric Eduardo. Wonderful local specialities include fried courgette flowers, ravioli stuffed with cheese and meat, and rabbit stew.

Hotels Nearby

Hotel Santa Caterina, Via Statale Amàlfitano, 84011 Amalfi, ✆ (089) 871012 (*expensive–moderate*).

Hotel Palazzo Murat, 84017, Positano, ✆ (089) 875177 (*moderate*), is a pretty 18th-century palace that has been converted into a comfortable hotel with a superbly peaceful garden.

Checklist

when to go

Late spring or **early autumn** is the best time to visit, when the weather is still glorious and the resorts have emptied considerably.

getting there

By air: British Airways fly to Naples twice daily from the UK; Alitalia fly to Naples from major European cities.

Transfers to and from Naples airport are available on request, otherwise take the Castellammare di Stabia exit off the motorway from the airport, and then take the Via Statale Amàlfitana 163 to Positano. Journey time is approximately 75 minutes.

tour operators

Packages to Le Sirenuse from the UK are available through **Elegant Resorts**, The Old Palace, Chester CH1 1RB, ✆ (01 244) 897 777.

booking direct

Reservations for Le Sirenuse can be made through **The Leading Hotels of the World**: from the UK, freefone ✆ (0800) 181 123; from the USA, toll-free ✆ (800) 223 6800.

entry formalities

US and Canadian citizens need full passports; a British Visitor's Passport is valid for up to 3 months' stay.

getting around

Car hire is advisable, and the major rental companies are represented at Naples airport.

getting by

The currency is the **Italian lira**. Major credit cards are accepted.

getting married

Marriages can be performed here.

114   *Italy: Positano*

Jersey: St Saviour

Longueville Manor
Longueville Road, St Saviour, Jersey JE2 7SA, Channel Islands
✆ (01534) 25501
✉ (01534) 31613
moderate

British honeymooners have been visiting Jersey in droves for over 40 years. And, without doubt, this appealing Channel Island, with its wide, sweeping sandy bays and its lush, forested and flower-filled interior, has much to offer couples looking for an affordable romantic retreat. It also enjoys a reasonably warm climate and has an abundance of excellent restaurants, nightclubs, pubs, watersports facilities and charming hotels.

Yet Jersey's reputation as the traditional honeymooners' island actually has little to do with romantic considerations; it dates back to the fifties, when significant tax breaks were offered to couples who married near the start of the financial year. In an aggressive marketing ploy, Jersey's hotels offered honeymooners similarly advantageous deals and the island quickly swelled with budget-minded sweethearts. There are stories of special honeymoon balls, of whole hotels taken over by couples and even of mass receptions held on the beaches. Today, perhaps mercifully, moderation prevails and the island's honeymooning reputation has been tempered by the influx of ordinary tourists.

Longueville Manor

There are beachside hotels full of character and cosy guest houses throughout the whole island but, for luxurious pampering in a relaxed and friendly atmosphere, Longueville Manor in the parish of St Saviour is the most inviting. One of Jersey's outstanding manor houses, Longueville belonged in medieval times to the island's reigning seigneurs. Its origins are 13th-century but much of this rambling stone house has been rebuilt or added later. There is an unusual Norman-style tower abutting the back of the hotel and some impressive 17th-century carved oak panelling in the dining-room and one of the sitting-rooms. To these historic remains the owners have made sympathetic additions: a modern wing housing generously proportioned bedrooms, a large heated swimming pool and, within the wooded lakeland grounds, tennis courts, kitchen gardens and greenhouses full of the brilliant blooms that decorate each room.

Private Comfort

The keynote in most of the 30 **bedrooms** is floral chintz, with rooms named after roses, and swagged curtains with matching wallpaper and plump cushions throughout. A more subdued decorative tone is to be found in **Pascali**, a pretty, light-filled attic room, large enough to be a called a mini suite, which overlooks the swimming pool and gardens.

The **garden suite** (one of Longueville's two suites) is the size of a substantial flat and has a private terrace with padded loungers, a drawing room with a dining-table and chairs and a conservatory. Paintings of ships, local guidebooks, colourful oriental rugs, antiques and good repro furniture embellish the bedroom and living-room, while the bathroom has a jacuzzi bath, outsized towels and a power shower.

Masquerade's bathroom is unashamedly romantic, with the bath set high on a dais and adorned with a chintz canopy, swept up into Hollywood-style swags and drapes. There are two four-poster bedrooms and even the smallest ordinary bedroom, **Apricot Silk**, is pleasantly restful and prettily decorated. Fresh flowers and mineral water are left in all rooms and replenished each day, and champagne is given to honeymooners.

Public Relaxation

Public areas of Longueville are invitingly cosy. The décor is smart but homely, with comfortable settees, open fireplaces, masses of magazines, antique *objets* and friendly, dozing cats who are willing to share sofa-space with guests. The hotel's dogs also add to the homely atmosphere: one of the two boxers will lead willing parties on walks around the grounds, while the other has perfected the art of looking endearing when either cakes or canapés appear on the scene.

Eating In

Longueville's young chef, **Andrew Baird**, has won awards for his cooking, and the food is certainly delicious The gourmet menu and the 3-course set menu change regularly, and the *table d'hôte* is immensely varied. The cuisine is light, with intelligent use made of **local produce**. **Shellfish**, from sweet-tasting scallops to lobster served with home-made pasta and basil, features heavily and such dishes as the ravioli of sweetbreads served with creamed morels illustrate the chef's imaginative approach to first courses. The staff are exceptionally helpful, courteous and friendly, and wines, including an array of champagnes, are served by the glass as well as the bottle.

What to See and Do

Although only 9 miles wide by 5 miles across, Jersey has around 50 miles of coastline, from sheltered coves and gentle sandy bays to dramatic craggy rocks and cliffs. Even in the height of summer it is easy to find empty secluded beaches, and the island is known for its clean bathing water, with 7 bays achieving the top '4 Dolphin' accolade in the Marine Conservation Society's 1995 *Good Beach Guide*. These **beaches** are: Archirondel, Beauport, Green Island, Greve de Lecq, Portelet, St Brelade and St Ouen. In the north the craggy coastline recalls parts of Devon and Cornwall; the part around **Rozel Bay** in the northeast is particularly enchanting, with deserted coves and dramatic cliff-faces. The tiny harbour next door is extremely picturesque, full of little beach huts, bobbing boats, old-fashioned bucket-and-spade shops and kiosks serving fresh crab sandwiches. Further east is Gorey Harbour sheltering traditional Victorian and Edwardian seaside buildings, and dominated by the impressive 13th-century **Mont Orgueil Castle**. Further still along the coast, a fine sandy beach marks the start of the **Royal Bay of Grouville**, and there are equally fine, sheltered beaches in the south at **St Brelade's** and **Ouaisne bays**.

Jersey is subject to huge tidal rises and falls, and it is necessary to plan beach trips keeping these in mind. Tides are high in the late mornings during the summer, and it is also best to check wind directions with hotel staff. **Watersports**, including **diving**, **surfing**, **water-skiing**, **yachting** and **windsurfing**, are all available. Contact the Jersey Seasport Centre at La Haule, St Aubin, ✆ 45040, or the Gorey Watersports Centre in Grouville, ✆ 853250.

St Helier is the capital town, and boasts two impressive covered markets selling fish and flowers, fruit and vegetables. The pedestrianized Halkett and Bath streets alongside the market have interesting gifts and clothes shops, brasseries and cafés. The lively **Jersey Museum** on Pier Road, ✆ 30511 (*open Mon–Sat, 10–5pm, Sun 1–5pm*), vividly evokes the history of the island. In particular, the *Occupation Tapestry*, woven by islanders to illustrate life under German rule, is certainly well worth viewing.

Inland, Jersey comprises lush wooded valleys, charming villages, shady lanes and open fields. **St Peter's Valley**, alongside the A11, is particularly enchanting and ideal for sheltered picnics and romantic walks or bicycle rides. The neighbouring **Living Legend Park**, rue du Petit Aleval, St Peter, ✆ 485496 (*open daily, 10–5.30pm during summer*), is a dynamic village-style attraction illustrating Jersey's rich heritage.

Also recommended is the **Hamptonne Country Life Museum**, rue de la Patente, St Lawrence, ✆ 863955 (*open daily, 10–5pm during summer*). Set in the heart of the countryside, this museum features painstakingly reconstructed medieval, 17th-century and Victorian dwellings, and working cider presses. The enterprising café sells picnic hampers complete with rug, drinks and sandwiches.

Day **trips by ferry** to the neighbouring Channel Islands of Guernsey, Sark and Herm, as well as to French coastal resorts such as Dinard and St Malo, are easy to arrange. Contact Channiland, ✆ (01534) 27088; Condor, ✆ (01305) 761551; or Emeraude Lines, ✆ (01534) 66566.

Eating Out

Jersey Pottery Restaurant, Gorey Village, Grouville, ✆ 851119 (*moderate; open lunchtime only, closed Sat and Sun*), is part of a huge local pottery complex, this plant-filled conservatory restaurant with outdoor seating serves remarkably good lobster, crab and *gambas* (large prawns) as well as fish dishes. The patisseries in particular are delicious and highly recommended.

The Village Bistro, Gorey Village, Grouville, ✆ 853429 (*inexpensive; closed Mon*), is a friendly and intimate bistro, serving dishes made from local produce.

Hotels Nearby

★★★★**Château la Chaire**, Rozel Bay, St Martin, ✆ (01534) 863354 (*moderate–inexpensive*), is an attractive country house hotel.

Checklist

when to go

Jersey looks at its best during the **summer,** when average temperatures are a pleasant 20°C. A number of festivals are held at this time: the Jersey Good Food Festival is held in June. In July there is the Jersey Floral Festival, and the famous Battle of Flowers begins on the first Thursday in August. September sees the launch of the Jersey World Music Festival. Further information on these events is available from Jersey Tourism, Liberation Square, St Helier, Jersey, ✆ (01534) 500777.

getting there

British Airways fly daily to Jersey from a number of UK airports. Flight time is 40 minutes; daily British Airways flights connect Paris and Jersey.

tour operators

Packages to Jersey from the UK mainland can be booked through **British Airways Holidays**, Astral Towers, Betts Way, London Road, Crawley, West Sussex RH10 2XA, ✆ (01293) 615353, and **Jersey Travel Service**, 45–57 London Road, Twickenham, Middlesex TW1 3TV, ✆ (0181) 891 6020. Packages include flights and car hire.

booking direct

From the USA, reservations for Longueville Manor can be made through the **Relais & Châteaux** New York Sales Office, ✆ (212) 8560115.

entry formalities

There is no passport control at Jersey. However, entry is via the UK, for which US and Canadian citizens need full passports.

getting around

Car hire is cheap and recommended, though **bicycles** are The major car rental companies are represented at Jersey Airport. C.I. Carriage Company, based in St Helier, ✆ 888700, offer a wide range of bicycles for hire.

getting by

The currency is the **Jersey pound**, but the **pound sterling** is accepted throughout Jersey. Major credit cards are accepted.

getting married

Marriages can be performed here.

Portugal: The Algarve

Hotel Quinta do Lago
Quinta do Lago, 8135 Almançil, The Algarve, Portugal
✆ (351 89) 396666
✉ (351 89) 396393
expensive

At the extreme southwestern corner of Europe and enjoying months of reliable sunshine, Portugal's Algarve has developed into a popular and often crowded holiday destination. But there are still some hidden gems along its beautiful coastline. If you hire a car it is easy to leave behind you the modern marinas and blandly international restaurants—and discover instead craggy cliffs and sandy coves, clear-water grottoes and small colourful fishing ports, and welcoming *casas de pasto* where succulent fish is cooked fresh from the sea.

For active couples the Algarve offers a wide range of sporting activities. The golf courses are among the finest in Europe, facilities for windsurfing, sailing and horseriding are numerous and tennis, fishing and waterskiing are readily arranged from most hotels.

Hotel Quinta do Lago

Hotel Quinta do Lago is in one of the most attractive resorts on this stretch of coastline. Just half an hour's drive away from Faro airport, it is part of a 1680-acre reserve of lakes, pools, lagoons, sand dunes and forests. Within this estate are a number of resorts with championship golf courses, country clubs, apartments and luxurious whitewashed holiday villas set in the vivid green, undulating landscape. The hotel is positioned alongside the Ria Formosa, a protected nature park comprising an enormous lagoon separated from the sea by sand dunes and salt-water marshes, a haven for rare species of sea birds and other flora and fauna.

The hotel's rooms overlook this vast, rather desolate estuary. The architecture is modern, the hotel's floors terraced into the landscape to form a pyramidal shape, with echoes of traditional Portuguese design evident in the red terracotta tiles, whitewashed walls and large, flower-filled balconies.

Private Comfort

This is a smart, comfortable, user-friendly hotel. **Bedrooms** are spacious, with vast picture windows overlooking the sea. And the **furnishings** are easy on the eye; predominantly pastel-coloured with pale wood detailing, they create a cool and relaxing environment. Honeymooners opting for the 3-night honeymoon programme (*from 128,750 escudos per couple*) are upgraded to a **suite**, where champagne and strawberries await their arrival and extras include use of the health club, a day's free car hire, a sunset carriage ride, and champagne cocktails with a candlelit dinner on the suite's terrace accompanied by a private guitar serenade.

Public Relaxation

The hotel has a pleasantly furnished and informal **bar** with an outdoor **terrace** where live music (usually classical and jazz guitar and vocals) is performed during warm evenings.

Eating In

There are two restaurants: the Ca' d'Oro serves reasonable **Italian** food, and the Navegadores, overlooking the outdoor pool, has a varied menu which includes traditional **Portuguese** dishes. Themed nights are staged here, with Portuguese performers inviting guests to perform fun and amusingly complicated traditional dance steps.

What to See and Do

Guests at the Quinta do Lago hotel can play **golf** at any of the resort's impressive courses and lessons are available for a reasonable fee. The hotel has its own **tennis courts**, again with tuition available, and there is a complex of **riding stables** with experienced instructors and a good range of horses to suit all levels of experience.

Scuba diving excursions to aircraft- and ship-wrecks can be arranged through the Watersports Centre, ✆(089) 394940. There is **windsurfing** on the estate's inland salt-water lagoon and swimming at the hotel's 2 pools or in the Atlantic itself. The beach is a short stroll away from the hotel, reached by a romantic wooden footbridge which crosses the estuary, at the end of which is Gigi's Restaurant and Bar. **Canoeing, windsurfing, body-boarding** (a form of horizontal surfing) and **jet-skiing** in the sea can all be arranged through Gigi's, ✆ (0676) 445178.

Bird-watching and the **nature trails** along the Ria Formosa are particularly rewarding, as is the São Lourenço nature trail—even for the sceptic who might ordinarily shun such pastimes. The guides are friendly and informative, and learning about the habits of little terns, spoon-billed waders, hoopoes and azure-winged magpies, and how to spot fiddler crabs and chameleons, makes an interesting change from more conventional sporting activities. Early morning is the best time to do the tour; the guides will pick guests up from the hotel.

Miltours travel agency, ✆ (089) 80 20 30, based in Faro, can arrange guided **tours** of the unspoilt regions of the Algarve either for couples alone or for small groups. The best tours cover the undeveloped areas east of Faro, and the beaches in this region are largely ignored by tourists. Long, sandy spits characterize the coast and provide relatively calm bathing; the wilder Atlantic beyond is for the strong, adventurous swimmer.

Almançil, lying inland from the hotel (about 15 minutes' drive north), is a pretty village of whitewashed homes arranged around the exquisite church of São Lourenço. Inside the church are some spectacular examples of Moorish-style blue-and-white *azulejos* (tiles) and, next door, a gallery sells local art and artefacts.

The holiday resort of **Vilamoura** is 20 minutes' drive west from Quinta do Lago. Moored in the marina is the **Condor de Vilamoura**, a replica sailing-galleon that can be chartered for afternoon cruises along the coastline. The hotel can book cruises, or you can ask at the Atlantico SA office in the marina.

Estói, 20 minutes' drive northeast of Quinta do Lago, has a fine Baroque church and a handsome square full of delicate lilac jacaranda trees, flanked by traditional pastel-painted homes. During the first week in May the villagers stage the spectacular Festa do Pinha (Pine Festival) when horsemen and women embellish their horses, saddlery and carts with flowers and palms, and parade through the streets in celebration of the commercial year.

Tavira, about 90 minutes' drive from the hotel, on the banks of the River Gilão, is well worth visiting. It has 37 churches topped by white domes and soaring spires, 16th- and 17th-century mansions and some very good fish restaurants along the river bank.

Faro has some attractive buildings within the old walled city. Grand squares, arcaded buildings, cobbled streets and orange trees create a peaceful haven away from the traffic. The centre of the town has a range of contemporary and international clothes stores, and in Rua Santo Antonio the enormous and traditional 1920s **Café Alicinça**, with its elaborate plaster ceiling, black and white photos of Old Faro and excellent ice-cream selection, is a good place to hang out.

Cacela Velha, about an hour's drive from Faro is a dreamy hamlet with a spectacular fort perched on a rock above a glorious white sand bar. Nearby, **Olhão** is a pretty, somewhat shabby little seaside town of cobbled streets and intensely coloured houses, with a marvellous old-fashioned covered market selling fish on one side, fruit, vegetables, honey, nuts and dried fruit on the other. Opposite the market are thoroughly Portuguese, decoratively tiled restaurants called *casas de pasto*. To these the fish of the day is brought from the market and cooked according to your specifications. Grilled fresh sardines and clams cooked in oil, garlic and parsley are particularly delicious.

Eating Out

Casa de Pasto 'O Bote', Avenida 5 de Outubro 122, ✆ (089) 72 11 83 (*inexpensive*), is great for fresh fish from the market and for *cataplana*—fish stew with prawns, clams, tomatoes and onions.

Gigi's Restaurant and Bar, at Quinto do Lago, is located opposite the hotel and over the wooden footpath (*moderate–inexpensive*). A lively and hospitable restaurant, it serves delicious lobster, giant prawns, grilled sea bass and salads.

Hotels Nearby

******Monte do Casal Country House Hotel**, Estói, Faro, is a small *pousada*-style country house hotel with tremendously pretty rooms.

Checklist

when to go

May and June are ideal months for visiting the Algarve, though **January and February**, when the almond blossom is abundant, are equally pleasant. During the spring, temperatures average a tolerable 25°C, the coastline is less crowded, the air is fresh and a wide variety of wild spring flowers are still in bloom.

tour operators

Packages, *pousadas* and fly–drives from the UK can be arranged with **Destination Portugal** at Madeira House, 37 Corn Street, Witney, Oxon OX8 7BW, ✆ (01993) 773269 and **Elegant Resorts**, The Old Palace, Chester CH1 1RB, ✆ (01 244) 897 777.

From the USA, packages to the Hotel Quinta do Lago can be organised through **Solar Tours**, 1629 'K' Street, 502, Washington DC 20006, ✆ (202) 861 5864, ✉ (202) 452 0905 and **Pinto Basios**, 40 Prince Street, New York, NY 10012, ✆ (212) 226 9056, ✉ (212) 966 1697.

booking direct

Reservations can be made through **Orient-Express Hotels** Sales Office: from the UK, ✆ (0171) 620 1210; from the US, ✆ (504) 522 5055 or toll-free ✆ (800) 237 1236. Also through the **Relais & Châteaux** New York Sales Office, ✆ (212) 8560115, or through **The Leading Hotels of the World**: from the UK, toll free ✆ (0800) 181 123; from the USA, toll-free ✆ (800) 223 6800.

entry formalities

US and Canadian citizens need full passports; a British Visitor's Passport is valid.

getting around

Car hire is recommended, available at Faro airport from the Autocerro desk in the arrivals hall. British Airways offer fly–drive packages.

getting by

English is spoken. The currency is the **escudo**. Major credit cards are accepted.

Scotland: Dunkeld

Kinnaird
Kinnaird Estate, by Dunkeld, Perthshire PH8 0LB, Scotland
© (01796) 482440
@ (01796) 482289
expensive –moderate

Perthshire is Scotland in microcosm—the country's most scenically varied district, where Highland meets Lowland—and a richly rewarding destination for motoring honeymoons. The region covers the wooded slopes and unspoilt broad valleys alongside the fast-flowing River Tay, including the dramatic Sma' Glen, and the peaceful expanse of Loch Leven with its island castle, once a lonely prison for Mary, Queen of Scots. During early summer and in autumn the hills of Perthshire reveal the inspiration behind the colours of the most famous Scots fabric, tweed. In the small historical centres of Pitlochry, Perth and Dunkeld, gratifyingly old-fashioned outfitters for timeless tweed jackets and tartan kilts echo the sedate atmosphere of the towns themselves.

Kinnaird

Kinnaird is a magically romantic hotel, full of character and atmosphere. The 18th-century grey stone dower house, clad in ivy and standing on a hill in an estate of over 9000 acres, enjoys unhindered views of the Tay Valley and the gentle hills of Amulree. It was built for the dashing mistress of the Duke of Atholl, and in the Edwardian era became a popular venue for Edwardian house parties. In 1927 it was purchased by the Hon. Lady Ward, and remained a family home until very recently. Though the house may look a little austere from the outside, the mood inside is relaxed and unstuffy, and the profusion of family ornaments, photographs, memorabilia and portraits helps keep it closer in spirit to a private residence than a 5-star hotel.

Private Comfort

Kinnaird appears imposingly large, but in fact it has just 8 double rooms and a suite. All the **bedrooms** are pleasingly spacious, retaining their handsome original proportions, with no attempt made to cram in extra rooms by chopping the largest in half. Each one is named after a cottage on the estate (these can be rented as an alternative to staying at the hotel), and the most pleasing are the corner rooms: Balmacneil, with its gargantuan bay window overlooking the estate, also boasts two massive sash windows either side of the bed, with soothing views of hillsides, river, woodland and valley as far as the eye can see. Pretty antique furniture includes a huge armoire with a chest of drawers below it, a somewhat worn cheval mirror, numerous prints of birds, and a handsome Adam-style fireplace, with a gas log fire beneath.

Like other bedrooms, Balmacneil is a deeply relaxing room which, though grand, invites the guest to feel at home. Nice touches include fresh flowers, a decanter of sherry alongside a tin of home-made shortbread, invitingly plump sofa and armchairs, and an appealing **teddy bear** dressed in a jumper and scarf resting on the pillows. The 'Kinnaird bear' is the hotel's individual interpretation of the 'do not disturb' sign.

Bathrooms are of a decent size and superbly old-fashioned, with large, thirties-style washbasins, a deep tub and enormous chrome shower-heads which positively drench the bather from head to toe.

Public Relaxation

Downstairs, Kinnaird's public rooms are equally inviting and look much as they would have done 80 years ago. The wood-panelled **drawing room**, with its big sash windows, Audubon bird prints and large crackling log fire, is where guests meet for drinks before dinner. Photographs of the Ward family (a member of whom currently owns the hotel) clutter the grand piano; there is a varied selection of magazines, backgammon sets and plenty of comfortable chairs and sofas. The more masculine **billiard room** is lined with glass cases holding the casts of numerous oversized salmon (some impressively weighing in at 50 pounds), all of which actually testify to the fishing prowess of female members of the Ward family.

Kinnaird's **grounds** are pleasingly unsophisticated, with the feel of a family garden, complete with **tennis courts**, **croquet lawn**, flowering plants, fruit trees and a **herb garden**. It is the sort of informal setting which inspires you to sit undisturbed under a tree with a good book. Pheasants and rabbits move freely through the grass, and in the evening the air is filled with vibrant birdsong, making way, as darkness falls, for the evocative hoot of an owl.

Eating In

Kinnaird's airy dining room is charmingly feminine. Antique panels painted in a rococo style depict pink-cheeked sweethearts besporting themselves in fantasy landscapes, while the large sash bay windows act as natural picture frames for the gentle moors outside. There is a set 3-course menu at £39.50 which includes mineral water, coffee and *petits fours*, and also VAT; the emphasis is placed on local ingredients like wild salmon poached in vegetables, deboned oxtail wrapped in cabbage, and succulent Aberdeen Angus beef.

Naturally, delicious buttered kippers feature on the **breakfast** menu.

What to See and Do

Kinnaird offers **salmon fishing** on the River Tay, near Dunkeld, on 2 beats, each extending for 3 miles. **Trout fishing** is available on 3 small lochs belonging to the estate, and the area is good for walking, shooting and bird-watching. All sorts of sports can be arranged. There are heated kennels in the grounds for gun-dogs, an all-weather **tennis court**, **horse-riding** locally, and **croquet** on the premises.

For gourmets, **Dunkeld Smoked Salmon**, Brae Street, Dunkeld, ✆ (01350) 727639, can arrange tastings as well as tours of the smokehouse.

Kinnaird is well placed for varied sightseeing. The bustling little town of **Pitlochry**, with its renowned Festival Theatre, salmon-ladder and woollen shops, is just 15 minutes away. Plays run from April through to October, and a full programme can be obtained from the Pitlochry Festival Theatre Box Office, ✆ (01796) 472680.

The smallest distillery in Scotland, **Edradour**, is just over 2 miles east of Pitlochry, ✆ (01796) 472095. Open daily from March through to October, they offer free tastings and guided tours, and there is a well-stocked shop of whisky-related items.

The hotel can arrange full- or half-day tours of **Perth** (22 miles from Kinnaird), and during May, Perth's Festival of the Arts stages concerts, Highland Nights and Scottish Ceilidhs throughout the city. The Perthshire Tourist Board, ✆ (01738) 638353, can provide more details of specific events.

One career couple chose a very grand Scottish hotel, converted from an ancient castle, for their all-too-brief honeymoon. Since it was out of season, the hotel was only too happy to upgrade them to the finest suite, but unfortunately their stay coincided with an impromptu visit from the Queen. Her Majesty needed somewhere to wash and brush up before attending a hastily organised reception in the main drawing room—and the honeymoon suite seemed the appropriate place. The couple agreed, little realizing just how disruptive the royal stop-over would prove. Early in the morning of their first day as Mr and Mrs, sniffer dogs were let loose in the suite. The couple had to pack up all their belongings and conceal their cases in another room, while engineers got down to the task of constructing a royal Portaloo. In retrospect they found the event highly amusing, but it was the insensitivity of the security team, rather than the hotel's deference to royalty, that niggled.

Three interesting historic **castles** are within easy reach of Kinnaird, all no more than 45 minutes' drive away, and each open daily from April through to October. **Scone Palace**, 2 miles northeast of Perth, ✆ (01738) 52300, was originally the place where Scottish kings were crowned, and is now a treasure-filled mansion house. **Glamis Castle**, off the A94, ✆ (01307) 840242, was the childhood home of the Queen Mother, and Duncan's Hall within the castle is the probable setting for Shakespeare's *Macbeth*. Neighbouring **Blair Castle**, off the A9, ✆ (01796) 481207, is the white-turreted seat of the Duke of Atholl, and its grounds and deer park are particularly fine.

Eating Out

★★★**East Haugh House**, East Haugh, by Pitlochry, ✆ (01796) 473121 (*moderate*), is a charming hotel with lunches and dinners served in the restaurant and conservatory bar. Fresh lobsters, scallops, mussels and local game are recommended.

★★★**Ailean Chraggan Hotel**, Weem, Aberfeldy, ✆ (01887) 820346 (*moderate–inexpensive*), has a good restaurant serving salmon and shellfish.

Hotels Nearby

★★★★**Cromlix House**, Kinbuck, by Dunblane, Perthshire, ✆ (01786) 822125. Couples can marry in the pretty neo-Gothic family chapel in the grounds of this 19th-century grey stone country house.

★★★★★**The Gleneagles Hotel**, Auchterarder, Perthshire, ✆ (01764) 662231, is a swish, luxurious twenties hotel with first-rate sport and spa facilities.

★★★**The Roman Camp**, Callander, Perthshire, ✆ (01877) 30003. Designed as a hunting lodge for the Dukes of Perth, this 17th-century hotel is near the site of a Roman encampment. It has a walled garden, and an informal atmosphere.

Cromlix House

Checklist

when to go

Scotland is appealing throughout the **summer**. In midsummer the evenings stay light until past 11pm. In June the landscape around Kinnaird looks most attractive, with bluebells, rhododendrons and wild roses. The weather, however, is unpredictable.

getting there

By air: Kinnaird is 90 minutes by road from Edinburgh and Glasgow airports. Both airports offer over 60 flights daily to the 3 London airports, as well as direct daily flights to regional airports, and some European destinations.

By road: Drive north of Dunkeld on the A9, exit left to B898 to Dalguise and Balnaguard. Kinnaird is just over 4 miles away, to the right.

By rail: Dunkeld and Pitlochry are the nearest railway stations, with links to Perth, Edinburgh and the north of England. The hotel is 15 minutes' drive from both stations, and guests can be met.

tour operators

Judy Peil Travel Inc., 147 North Meramec Avenue, Saint Louis, Missouri 63105, ✆ (314) 726 2577, ✉ (314) 726 2128, arrange holidays for US honeymooners. Bargain winter breaks are available.

booking direct

From the USA, reservations can be made through the **Relais & Châteaux** New York Sales Office, ✆ (212) 8560115.

getting around

Car hire is recommended. The hotel can arrange car hire for guests, or try Highland and Perthshire Tourist Services Ltd in Pitlochry, ✆ (01796) 473066.

entry formalities

US and Canadian citizens need full passports.

getting by

The currency is the **pound sterling**. Scottish and English currency are interchangeable. Major credit cards are accepted.

getting married

Marriages can be performed here.

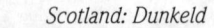

Scotland: Dunkeld

The Seychelles

L'Archipel
Anse Gouvernement
Praslin, The Seychelles
✆ (00 248) 232242
📠 (00 248) 232072
expensive–moderate

La Digue Island Lodge
La Digue, The Seychelles
✆ (00 248) 234233
📠 (00 248) 234100
moderate

Denis Island
Denis Island, PO Box 404,
Victoria, Mahe, The Seychelles
✆ (00 248) 3421143
📠 (00 248) 3421010
expensive

The Seychelles: Praslin

The second-largest island in the hundred or so islands that make up the Seychelles archipelago, Praslin measures just 11km by 8km. Its proximity to the capital island of Mahe (37km northeast, accessible by air in 15 minutes) as well as to neighbouring La Digue makes this a good base for island-hopping. Island link-ups, either by ferry or air, can be arranged independently or through your hotel, often on the day you wish to travel. Even so, it is a very good idea to stay put for three or more nights on one island, since the Seychelles should be enjoyed at a slower pace; its natural beauty needs to be savoured. Diving and snorkelling are excellent; the islands have unspoilt coral reefs, teeming with tropical fish.

Praslin is more sophisticated than the other islands, but still rich in natural beauty. Visitors here can choose to be solitary or to socialize: for those seeking company, there is a fairly lively stretch of beaches with fun bars, good hotels and friendly restaurants along the Golden Coast in the northwest.

L'Archipel

L'Archipel is tucked away on a quiet corner of the Golden Coast with its own small but sheltered beach, called Anse Gouvernement. The pleasant architecture of the resort blends sympathetically with the natural contours of the landscape.

Private Comfort

Accommodation is in 22 individual **cottages** nestling in the hillside, rising in terraces from the beach; each has a view of the bay. The **furnishings** are attractively modern in Scandinavian style, with gleaming wood panelling, floors and furniture. The double beds are low-level, with muslin mosquito netting gathered up into a rosette during the day and draped over the bed at night. The spacious rooms are kept cool with air-conditioning and ceiling fans. **Balconies** are large and secluded from neighbours, and **bathrooms** are well equipped with showers, good-quality towels, soaps and scented bath gels. All cottages have a television, safe and minibar.

Eating In

There is a beach bar to the left of the sandy bay where guests can get cold drinks (the creamy fruit punches are superb), club sandwiches, chips and salads during the day. The main 'lodge', with its comfortable rattan sofas and armchairs decorated in tropical fabrics, houses a first-rate restaurant upstairs. This is open-fronted, with most of the candlelit tables arranged so that guests can look out to sea as they dine. When the sun has set and the evening rains have washed the resort clean, it is magical to sit here and watch the progress of a night-time storm as it noisily sweeps from glistening palm to empty beach. The cicadas are silent, and the breezes that make the candles flicker in their storm lanterns provide a refreshing waft of cool air for the diners.

The cooking at L'Archipel is of a high standard, featuring local produce and cooking techniques. Typical dishes include steamed parrotfish with cucumber, fish curries and clean-tasting fruit sorbets and ice-creams.

What to See and Do

At the hotel, watersports include **canoeing** and **snorkelling**, and the staff are happy to arrange excursions around the island to its renowned beauty spots or to other beaches.

The most famous of these beauty spots is the **Vallée de Mai** (*open daily 8–4.30pm*), a dense 45-acre forest located southeast of the hotel, off the road running from Grand Anse to Baie Sainte Anne. This vast, unspoilt forest has many different plants, and palm trees that grow to a staggering 47 feet high. When the wind whips through these giants and the massive palm fronds thrash against each other, the sound of leaves creaking, groaning and slapping, together with the haunting cry of the black parrot is quite eerie. General Gordon of Khartoum visited the Vallée a century ago and declared that it was the original Garden of Eden, when he saw the **Coco de Mer**—the enormous coconut which resembles a plump female's bottom and pelvis. The origin and powers of this strange fruit have been puzzled over for centuries. Philosophers believed it was the fruit of the Tree of Knowledge; sailors and explorers thought it must grow under the sea, on account of the fact that it floated as far as the Maldives; and because of its womanly shape it also gained a reputation as an aphrodisiac. A visit to the Vallée de Mai to see these bizarre coconuts, and the giant palms that bear them, is a must.

There are ferry excursions to nearby **Cousin Island**, which lies off the southwest coast of Praslin, on Tuesdays, Thursdays and Fridays. One of the smallest inhabited islands at just 1km across, Cousin Island is home to 6 humans and a vast array of rare land and sea birds. The excursion guides provide a fascinating tour: among the resident fauna are George and Tina the centenarian tortoises and various birds, including the Seychelles fody, fairy terns, Seychelles turtle doves, noddies, and white-tailed tropical birds which make their nests in the roots of trees. Hawksbill turtles also live here; their young are helped along into the sea by the local guides, to save them from the greed of the local ghost crabs.

Eating Out

Les Rochers, Grosse Roche, La Pointe, Praslin, © (00 248) 233034 (*moderate*), is a superb restaurant with a stunningly unspoilt beach-side setting. Specialities include garlic and curry prawns, slipper lobster, aubergine fritters and warm octopus salad.

Hotels Nearby

Paradise Hotel, Côte d'Or, Praslin, © (00248) 232255 (*moderate–inexpensive*).

The Seychelles: La Digue

Visiting La Digue, the fourth-largest island in the Seychelles, is like entering a time-warp. Only six cars are allowed to use its makeshift roads, and then only for transporting goods to the islanders. Shops are small and basic, important meeting centres as well as places for stocking up on provisions. And the schoolchildren, immaculate in their neat uniforms, actually sing hymns in the playground rather than pop songs. The women still dry their laundry on rocks in the sunshine, and most locals and visitors get around on rusty and cranky bicycles, or ox-drawn carts.

Just like its transport system, life on La Digue moves slowly, and it pays to adjust yourself to the pace. This is an extremely pretty island, with simple, colourful villages comprising traditional wooden Seychellois houses with wraparound verandahs painted in bright primary colours, a church next to the local school, and an open-air bar and shop. Fronting these hamlets, and sheltered by huge granite rocks, are some of the best beaches in the Seychelles, with sand as soft as talcum powder, warm, clear water and very few visitors.

La Digue Island Lodge

There are plenty of comfortable small properties, from bungalows to guest houses, along the west coast of La Digue. In contrast to some of the larger resorts on the capital island of Mahe, these properties offer an authentic taste of island living, for furnishings, food, entertainment and service all mirror the traditional Seychellois way of life. La Digue Island Lodge is the best known of these properties: well established, and with a supremely peaceful setting among coconut palms and flowering shrubs, a large open-air restaurant overlooking La Réunion beach and, in the distance, the island of Praslin.

Private Comfort

Accommodation ranges from romantic tent-style A-frame **chalets**, most of which are set right on the beach, to cosy thatched **rondavels** sheltering between towering palms. Both are ideal for couples, and enjoy private **showers** and air-conditioning.

Part of the same property is the **Yellow House**, located across the lane from the lodge. This is a converted plantation house with pale lemon wooden walls and white shutters, and has clean, simple, airy **bedrooms** each with a private shower and bath. One-bedroom sea-facing **suites** are also available.

Public Relaxation

The family-run lodge has a homely, friendly atmosphere, with guests gathering in the open-air **lounge** throughout the day. There is a small **boutique** selling souvenirs, suntan oil, *pareos*, postcards and snacks; **snorkelling**, as well as **fishing** and **diving** trips, and **visits to neighbouring islands** are organised by staff. There is a **swimming pool**, and La Réunion **beach**, which fronts the hotel, is sheltered and clean, with soft sand and comfortable recliners.

Eating In

Seychellois food is delicious, spicy and with a **fishy** emphasis. The restaurant at La Digue Island Lodge serves **Creole** specialities at both lunch and dinner.

What to See and Do

During the day, La Digue takes on the appearance of a tropical Cambridge, with hordes of bikes parked against buildings, and bicyclists crowding the narrow lanes. There are some gentle hills where the breathless might wish to dismount and walk for a while; otherwise this is a manageable island, even for the lazy. Despite being the fourth-largest island, La Digue measures only 3km by 5km, so it is easy to tour its boundaries by **bike** (*see* 'Checklist' below) or even on foot.

The island is famed for its faultless **beaches**, the best of which are along the west coast, from Pointe Cap Barbi in the northwest, down to Anse Pierrot. Three-quarters of the way down the coast, Pointe Source d'Argent and Pointe St Jacques further south boast some breathtakingly dramatic rock formations: vast blocks of granite, uncannily like Henry Moore sculptures, changing in colour from pale rose to elephant grey as the day progresses. The east coast is the most savage, and the beaches there are often plagued by strong currents but, even so, the area is worth visiting for its striking landscape.

La Digue will hold immense appeal for **naturalists**. It is home to the tiny and relatively rare **black paradise flycatcher**, so named because of its flamboyant black feathers and extended beak. Unusual species of **crabs** are found on the beaches, and if you are lucky you might spot the bizarre **periophthalamus**, a bug-eyed creature that is a cross between a fish and a mammal and thought to be one of the oldest vertebrates known to man.

Shells are beautifully intricate, varied and abundant. The best can be found around Anse Sévère and Anse Gaulettes up in the remote north. Look and admire, but do not steal them away.

Wild orchids grow along the hedgerows, and in the woody, lush interior of the island the air is rich with the sweet smells of vanilla and patchouli. Both of these vie with the acrid fumes emanating from the **copra** factory. Located at l'Union, a 10-minute bike ride from the Lodge, the factory is interesting to visit as it shows how, apart from tourism, the locals make their living. It is located in an old plantation house and working farm where vanilla pods are processed ready for export, alongside hundreds of drying coconut husks which are later crushed for their oil and pulped for animal food.

Eating Out

Restaurant Patatran, Anse Patate, ✆ (00 248) 234333 (*expensive*), serves local specialities like crab curry cooked in coconut milk, and fish stew. From the open-air room upstairs, the restaurant has good views northwards towards the island of Felicité, now an annexe to La Digue Island Lodge, with similar accommodation. For a honeymoon hideaway with a difference, the island can be rented out to a minimum of 2 and up to a maximum of 8 people; minimum stay 3 days. All enquiries to La Digue Island Lodge.

Hotels Nearby

Choppy's Bungalows, Anse Réunion, La Digue, The Seychelles, ✆ (00 248) 234224.

The Seychelles: Denis Island

With 350 acres of lush jungle, a handful of comfortable thatched cottages, the warmth of a clear, clean Indian Ocean, dazzling in its aquamarine intensity and fringed with the finest powder-white sand, Denis is one of the Seychelles' most peaceful islands, favoured for its tranquillity by stars such as Catherine Deneuve and Charlotte Rampling.

Denis Island

Denis Island's simple landing strip is just 25 minutes by air from the capital island of Mahe. Your first glimpse of the island from above is unforgettable. Like a vast green comma printed on a turquoise sheet of water, its edges fringed with coral reefs, Denis Island looks completely deserted from the air. Yet those lush coconut trees conceal a small village, a farm, two prisons (no longer functioning), an open-air ecumenical chapel and 24 spacious guest cottages, nestling along the curve of the island's most sheltered beach.

When the tiny plane that brings you here lands, its 8 passengers are greeted by a welcome parade. The island's local children hang around Customs (a palm-capped shelter equipped with benches and a weighing machine), expressions of curiosity and glee on their guileless faces. Two beautiful Denis Island girls, clad in colourful sarongs, with fragrant frangipani woven into their hair, greet new guests and escort them to an large, open-plan, breezy lodge, the club house where fellow islanders meet for cocktails and dinner, lunch and parties with live music.

The island is the brainchild of French industrialist Pierre Burkhardt: a lively, diminutive figure, who initially kept Denis as a private retreat for family and friends. It was Pierre who invented 'Denis time'; the island is an hour ahead of the rest of the Seychelles.

Private Comfort

Accommodation is in **cottages**, cleverly placed so that each one is completely private. The wide verandahs offer a view of sand and sea; you can lie in your bath, bathroom doors open on to the verandah, and be cooled by the gentle breezes wafting through the palms, while watching the sun hitting the ocean's dazzling green surface.

Bedrooms are large and sheltered from the elements by louvred wooden doors. **Furnishings** are simple and in local style: a colourful woven rug, a plain table and chair, a bamboo wardrobe and a comfortable double bed crowned with a white froth of mosquito netting. Denis Island will particularly suit those who like the simple life: ceiling fans cool each cottage, but don't expect hi-tech air-conditioning.

In the **bathroom**, as you clean your teeth you might find yourself staring into the eye (or is it the mouth?) of a black millipede as fat as your thumb and twice as long, and the showers outside are much-favoured as a watering hole by the island's 150 giant tortoises. A note in each cottage firmly but politely points out that 'creepy-crawlies, beatles [sic] and spiders' are part of the island life and adds that, should they offend, the management will do everything in their power to assist you off Denis Island 'as quickly as possible'.

One couple decided to avoid the stress of a big wedding by getting married in the Seychelles. The hotel laid on a ceremony in the garden, witnesses, champagne and a beautiful cake. The cake and champagne were displayed on a table beside the flower-garlanded arch under which the bride and groom exchanged their vows. Halfway through the ceremony, guests saw the hotel's dog, a tubby mongrel, trot past. A few moments later, chomping sounds rose from the direction of the table. Bride, groom and minister continued stoically with the service. When at last the couple were lawfully wed, they turned to see what had happened. The was no sign of the dog, or the cake.

Apparently the hotel conducted an average of 3 weddings per week. The groom wasn't surprised. It was obvious now why the dog was so fat...

Guests are encouraged to set their own pace. If peace and privacy is your priority no one will disturb you here. Indeed, you can easily spend days without meeting another guest. But if you choose company, then the clubby restaurant-bar is just a few sandy footsteps away from your cottage.

Eating In

In the restaurant-bar are served the most mouthwatering of **Creole**-based buffet lunches and dinners; fish curries cooked in lime, saffron and coconut, salads of palm heart with a light vinaigrette and dreamy creamy home-made vanilla-flavoured puddings, washed down with exotically potent **cocktails**.

What to See and Do

Most guests divide their day between **sunbathing, swimming, snorkelling, windsurfing** and trips in the lodge's **glass-bottomed boat**, with the odd snooze thrown in during the heat of the afternoon.

You can walk around the island's coast in a couple of hours and are very likely to see no sign of life, save for the startled side-scuttle of a ghost crab as it panic-runs back to its sandy base. And solitary **walks** through the jungly interior are fascinating for nature lovers. Snowy terns, in their curiosity, fly close to your face; the air is rich with the hauntingly mesmeric cooing of the ground dove and eerie rustlings from unseen insects, noises that vie with the undercurrent rumble of distant waves. You will probably come across one of the island's giant tortoises. Leathery crow's-feet frame the all-knowing eyes of a reptile that may be up to 180 years old.

You can emerge from the jungle into the island farm and village and then take the dusty road leading to the pretty open-air chapel where Parisian jeweller Cartier's daughter was married, in the late eighties, by a French cardinal in front of a handful of chic Parisian guests.

At an additional cost, you can go **deep-sea fishing**. Even the amateur angler should try his hand at tuna fishing. The catch will probably only consist of a bonito fish or two, but you may just hook a barracuda. Many guests brag about their catch of an 80lb sailfish, even though the boatman is often the one who has put in the hard work!

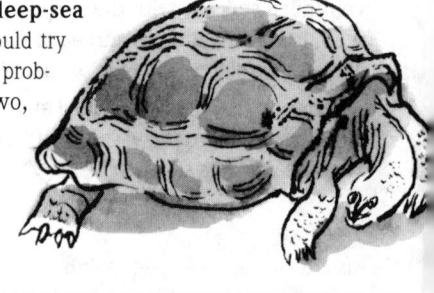

Hotels Nearby

Bird Island Lodge, Bird Island, ✆ (00 248) 224925 (*expensive*).

Château d'Eau, PO Box 107, Barbarons, Mahe, ✆ (00 248) 378577 (*moderate*).

Auberge Louis XVII, PO Box 607, La Louise, Mahe, ✆ (00 248) 344411 (*moderate*). Both of these are charming, traditionally furnished small guest houses.

Checklist

when to go

The weather in the Seychelles is generally warm and humid. The driest months run from **May to September**. Showers are heaviest from December to February, and these months are better avoided. During the summer, seaweed collects on Praslin's Grand'Anse beach in the southeast, so it is best to book a hotel on the northwest coast.

getting there

By air: Air Seychelles fly twice a week from London to Mahe, with connections to Paris, Frankfurt, Madrid, Johannesburg, Singapore, Dubai and Nairobi. British Airways offer two non-stop flights a week from London. Aeroflot, Air France and Kenya Airways also serve the Seychelles.

From the capital island of Mahe, Air Seychelles operates daily scheduled inter-island flights. The journey time to Praslin is 15 minutes; the fare is £55 return. You can fly from Mahe to Denis Island on Sundays, Tuesdays, Thursdays and Fridays. The cost is approximately £100 return.

By ferry: La Digue Island is only accessible by daily ferry—journey time is 3 hours from the capital island of Mahe (£30 return), and 30 minutes from Praslin (£10 return).

tour operators

In the UK, Kuoni, 33 Maddox St, London W1R 9LD, ✆ (01303) 226605 and Tropical Places, Freshfield House, Lewes Road, Forest Row, East Sussex RH18 5ES, ✆ (01342) 825123, offer packages to **Praslin**.

Reservations for **La Digue** can be made through Airwaves, 10 Bective Place, London SW15 2PZ, ✆ (0181) 875 1188. 954 1944.

British Airways Holidays, Astral Towers, Betts Way, London Road, Crawley, West Sussex RH10 2XA, ✆ (01293) 611611 and Elegant Resorts, The Old Palace, Chester CH1 1RB, ✆ (012 44) 897 888, offer packages to **Denis Island**.

Praslin, **La Digue** and **Denis Island** can be booked through Tropical Places, Freshfield House, Lewes Road, Forest Row, East Sussex RH18 5ES, ✆ (01342) 825123.

In the USA, bookings for **Praslin**, **La Digue** and **Denis Island** can be made with Abercrombie & Kent International Inc., 1420 Kensington Road, Oak Brook, Illinois 60521, ✆ (312) 954 1944.

entry formalities

UK and US and Canadian citizens need full passports and return tickets.

health

Immunization against cholera, typhoid, polio and hepatitis A is recommended. Sterilize drinking water.

getting around

A mini moke is the best means of transport around **Praslin**. Try Standard Car Hire, Anse Kerlan, ✆ (00 248) 233555.

On **La Digue**, hiring a bike is easy, fun and a cheap way of sightseeing (around £3/$5 a day). They are available from the pier, to the right as you disembark from the ferry. Ox-carts are an amusing way of viewing the island, but you might get slightly frustrated at the lack of speed—save them for a lazy afternoon transfer between beaches.

getting by

The main language is **French**, though English is widely spoken. The currency is the **Seychellois rupee** (SR), which is divided into 100 cents. Major credit cards are accepted.

getting married

Marriages can be performed here.

South Africa: *Blue Train*

From Cape Town to Johannesburg
on the *Blue Train*
expensive

South Africa has been called 'a world in one country' because it combines a variety of cosmopolitan cities with diverse countryside, mountain resorts, spectacular plains and coastal regions, and game reserves rich in wildlife. This diversity makes it a country that is nearly impossible to get to know within a short amount of time. So the ideal visit would include some degree of city sightseeing and either a safari or a stay on one of the pristine beaches on the Indian Ocean. For honeymooners with limited time to explore, a trip on the luxurious *Blue Train*, which covers 1500km of South African countryside, provides a taste of the beautiful southwestern Cape, the wide open spaces of the central, landlocked Orange Free State and two fascinating cities: Cape Town and Johannesburg.

Blue Train

The famous *Blue Train* which travels from Cape Town to Johannesburg in 24 hours across the most spectacular South African countryside, is a 5-star hotel and restaurant on wheels. Built in the seventies, the *Blue Train* was designed with attention to every detail of passengers' comfort: a thin layer of gold on the double-glazed windows helps to reduce glare; there are electrically operated Venetian blinds to ward off the daytime sun; and pneumatic suspension ensures a smooth and quiet ride.

While the hundred-odd passengers check in at the designated lounge in Cape Town station, their luggage is swiftly stowed in their cabins. Sightseers and relatives come along to wave the train off, and the sense of excitement as the 16-car train pulls out of the station is similar, one imagines, to the thrill felt at the celebrated departures of the old ocean-going liners.

Private Comfort

The checking-in procedure is quick and efficient and once on board you feel welcome immediately: in your cabin you will find thoughtful touches such as a washbag filled with shower gels and soaps, a half-bottle of champagne, flowers and mineral water.

The **cabins** are pleasingly old-fashioned and surprisingly spacious, with teak furniture and fittings and pink and blue patterned fabrics. **Beds** are made up with crisp cream linen sheets and there is a choice between cabins with (rather narrow) single beds and those with double beds. Each cabin has a washbasin; the showers are down the corridor but there are plans to install *en suite* bathrooms soon. For greater luxury, there is a 3-room **suite**, complete with bedroom, bathroom and living room—wallowing in a bath while travelling at 100km an hour is an experience not to be missed.

Stewards look after the same couples throughout the journey; their duties include pressing passengers' clothes before dinner, tidying up cabins, serving morning tea or coffee and preparing snacks.

Public Relaxation

The atmosphere on board the *Blue Train* is generally highly sociable, with the mostly British, American and European passengers meeting before and after meals, either in the **bar car** or the **lounge**. Both these areas are decorated with elaborate displays of African flowers such as orchids, protea and strelitzia, and furnished with comfortable bar chairs and sofas.

Eating In

The cooking on board is of a high standard and the portions are generous. Unlimited drinks are included in the price of the trip, and lunch and dinner are 6-course affairs with a choice given for each course. It is worth eating at the more leisurely second sitting to avoid feeling rushed or forced to eat too early in the evening. Typical dishes include locally caught crayfish appetizers, duck and lamb main courses and imaginatively presented, delicious puddings all served on tables set with crystal and silver tableware on pink and white linen and eaten in the light of tiny glowing lamps.

What to See and Do

It pays to spend a few days in **Cape Town**, perhaps in Mount Nelson Hotel (*see* p.149), and to explore the **Cape Peninsula** before boarding the *Blue Train*. The city is an eclectic mix of meticulously preserved Edwardian and Victorian architecture and modern buildings, cobblestoned streets with little boutiques and elegant shopping malls with art galleries. The city has a most distinctive setting: the well-known backdrop of Table Mountain dominates the peninsula, which is punctuated by pretty bays, sheltered beaches of dazzling white sand and small fishing villages.

Hire a car and head for the dramatic **Cape of Good Hope**. The most popular panoramic drive is from Simon's Town through the Cape of Good Hope Nature Reserve, which has an enormous natural wild flower garden, and on to Cape Point. From here, on a clear day, you can see beyond False Bay, with its miles of tantalizing beaches, to the other side of the peninsula.

The top of **Table Mountain** offers the best view of the city and beyond. Take the thrilling, shaky, 7-minute Table Mountain aerial cable, and spend time roaming on

One couple booked a beautiful-looking and very pricey hotel on the strength of a brochure. When they got there they found that the sash windows were draughty and rattled at the slightest breeze, the heavily chintzed 'dressing table' concealed a rickety mess of plywood and staples underneath, and, worst of all, the bedsprings were ancient and creaky beneath the crisply ironed sheets and flounced floral pillowcases. The hotel is now in the hands of receivers...

the rocky summit. Maps and telescopes are provided to help visitors get their bearings and if the weather deteriorates a warning signal is sounded.

The 10km journey from Cape Town along **Chapman's Peak Drive** is equally spectacular. There are views over Chapman's Bay to pretty harbours like Hout Bay, a working port filled with fishing fleets that trawl the waters for succulent crayfish.

Once aboard the *Blue Train*, armchair sightseeing begins with the **Paarl vineyards**, one of the best wine-producing areas in South Africa. Next, about 150km from Cape Town, there is a brief stop in the tiny, well-preserved Victorian town of **Matjiesfontein**. Originally the military headquarters of the British Forces during the Boer War, it is now exclusively a tourist attraction. The interesting museum and Lord Milner pub are both well stocked with a variety of memorabilia relating to the town's past.

During the remaining daylight hours, the train travels slowly and will pause at specific beauty spots so that photographs can be taken. At night, it gathers pace in order to cover the ground to Johannesburg. On the following morning, your journey takes you across the desert landscape of the Orange Free State, with its majestic mountains and mile upon mile of brown scrubland. From time to time, the track curves so sharply that the train bends into a 'U' and photographers on board can snap the front and rear of the train from the middle.

Finally, the *Blue Train* pulls into **Johannesburg**. Southwest of the railway station is **Gold Reef City**, a popular reconstruction of pioneer Jo'burg during the gold rush, where visitors dressed in protective hats and raincoats can see a 'gold pour' and descend a 220-metre mine shaft.

Johannesburg is within easy reach of some of the country's finest game reserves. The **Kruger National Park** is 4 hours' drive from the city, or 45 minutes by scheduled flight with South African Airways.

Hotels Nearby

Mount Nelson Hotel, 76 Orange Street, Cape Town 8001, ✆ (027) 21 23 1000, ✉ (027) 21 24 7472 (*expensive*), is Cape Town's famous pastel pink Edwardian grand hotel. Set apart from the main building in private gardens are 8 suites fashioned from a row of beautifully restored historic cottages. An Orient-Express Hotel, reservations can be made by calling toll-free ✆ (800) 237 1236.

Sandton Sun, on the corner of Alice and 5th Streets, Sandton, Johannesburg, ✆ 780 5000 (*expensive*), is an ultra-modern, luxury hotel.

Connect With

L'Archipel, Praslin, The Seychelles (*see* pp.134–136).
La Digue Island Lodge, La Digue, The Seychelles (*see* pp.136–139).
Denis Island, The Seychelles (*see* pp.139–144).

Checklist

when to go

Midwinter, which runs from **June to August**, is the most pleasant time for visitors, when the climate ranges from Mediterranean-style mildness in the Cape Peninsula to sub-tropical weather in the coastal resorts.

getting there

From the UK: British Airways and South African Airways have regular scheduled flights to Cape Town's D.F. Malan Airport. KLM (via Amsterdam) and Lufthansa (via Germany) also fly to Cape Town.

From the USA: The offices of SAA are at 900 Third Avenue, New York, ✆ (212) 826 0995, or toll-free ✆ (800) 722 9675, with flights from the USA via Johannesburg's Jan Smuts International Airport, connecting to Cape Town. Africa Direct fly from Atlanta.

tour operators

From the UK, packages are available with **Sunset Travel Holidays**, 4 Abbeville Mews, Clapham Park Road,

London SW4 7BX, © (0171) 498 9922, and **The African Experience**, 278 Battersea Park Road, London SW11 3BS, © (0171) 924 4008. From the USA, book with **Abercrombie & Kent International Inc.**, 1520 Kensington Road, Oakbrook, IL 60521, © (708) 954 2944.

booking direct

For independent bookings on *The Blue Train*, call © (0 27) 11 773 76 31.

entry formalities

UK and US citizens need full passports.

health

Immunization against cholera, typhoid, polio, hepatitis A, and antimalarial tablets are recommended. Sterilize drinking water. Rabies and bilharzia are present in some areas.

getting around

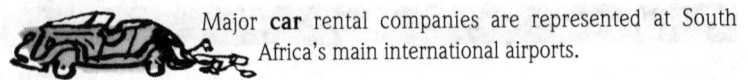

Major **car** rental companies are represented at South Africa's main international airports.

getting by

English is widely spoken. The currency is the **rand**, which is divided into 100 cents. Major credit cards are accepted.

USA: San Francisco

Mandarin Oriental
222 Sansome Street, San Francisco, CA 94104, USA
✆ (415) 885 0999
✉ (415) 433 0289
expensive

San Francisco might well be considered one of the most appealing cities in the USA. It has a spectacular setting on the hilly tip of a peninsula, with the Pacific on one side and 'The Bay', one of the world's largest natural harbours, on the other. It is also a city full of visual contradictions. Skyscrapers meet with 'Painted Ladies', the pretty pastel-coloured Victorian homes of the mission district; and vibrant Chinatown, truly a city within a city, is an enormous chaotic enclave at the heart of downtown's ordered financial district. San Francisco can be explored on foot in just a few days, and is also well placed for trips along the scenic Pacific coast.

Mandarin Oriental

San Francisco has some first-rate hotels, ranging from luxury to inexpensive, and including interesting 'boutique' hotels. These are essentially small establishments, elegantly furnished, often with antiques, where importance is placed on personal service. Within the expensive category, the Mandarin Oriental provides a most enthralling base for a honeymoon. The hotel occupies the top 11 floors of the twin-towered First Interstate Center, a mixed-use development located in the financial district. As San Francisco's third-tallest building, it towers high above the skyline; each floor is connected by a glass sky-bridge which, like the bedrooms and suites, provides truly breathtaking panoramas of the city.

Private Comfort

The corner '**Mandarin Rooms**' are quite the most covetable in the hotel. Full-length picture windows flank two walls of these suite rooms, providing dramatic and unobstructed views over San Francisco to the Bay and the Golden Gate Bridge. Here you can enjoy a lazy American breakfast in bed, promptly and elegantly served with a red rose and on white linen, while gazing across the skyline at hundreds of faceless office windows and savouring the contrast between your secluded luxury and the bustle of the everyday working world.

In keeping with the ethos of the Mandarin Oriental Hotel Group, **furnishings** throughout are stylishly minimalist, with a strong Oriental accent. The Mandarin Rooms are painted a subtle lemon tone, and have pale wood room-dividers to create an elegant sitting area with cream sofas and a coffee table. Newlyweds are greeted with champagne and fresh fruit, and welcome touches include delicious cookies, a snack basket, cotton Mandarin Oriental yukata bathrobes and slippers. Hotel stationery, personalised with the guests' names picked out in gold, provides a fun and swanky way to finish off those wedding gift thank-yous.

King-size **beds** are supremely comfortable, and the spacious **bathrooms** are staggeringly luxurious. Terracotta-coloured marble extends from floor to ceiling; twin basins, walk-in power showers and a deep tub are set alongside an enormous picture window. You can lie in a luxuriously foamy bath, looking directly across to the soaring pyramid of the TransAmerica Tower, with views of the Golden Gate Bridge beyond. Aeroplanes appear at eye-level, fluffy clouds waft by—the panorama, and indeed the whole 'Mandarin experience', is cinematic in its variety and richness.

Eating In

The hotel's restaurants include the Mandarin Lounge, for light meals and afternoon teas, and 'Silks', located on the second floor. Here, stylish works of contemporary art hang on the walls, and the cuisine theme is **Californian** dining with an **Asian** accent—essentially, dishes are edible works of art with a spicy edge.

What to See and Do

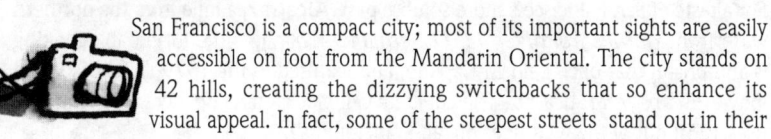

San Francisco is a compact city; most of its important sights are easily accessible on foot from the Mandarin Oriental. The city stands on 42 hills, creating the dizzying switchbacks that so enhance its visual appeal. In fact, some of the steepest streets stand out in their own right as sights worth seeing—at their summit, the tallest downtown skyscrapers are almost dwarfed by the sharp gradients. Crookedest Street, for example, between Hyde Street and Leavenworth Street near Russian Hill, snakes down a slope steep enough to put the fear of God into an experienced skier. Some of these hills are pretty exhausting to climb, so it's as well that San Francisco's public transport system is reliable and easy to use.

For walking expeditions, the area around **Alamo Square** is worth exploring. This quiet residential neighbourhood is full of spectacular converted Victorian houses, which give it a decidedly European atmosphere. **Telegraph Hill** has quite the best views of the city and is also a good area for fashionably chic restaurants. The climb is rewarding—the air is fresh, with very little noise from the city to spoil the vivid sense of San Francisco's past. On the harbour slopes of the hill stand pretty clapboard cottages, surrvivors of the 1906 earthquake and fire. These cottages have impressive flower-filled gardens or balconies spilling bright red geraniums, bougainvillaea and jasmine, and are only accessible via rickety wooden walkways and steps. With their prime position overlooking the bay, they became a magnet for artists and at one time that area was known as the 'Art Colony'.

At the summit of Telegraph Hill stands **Coit Tower** (*open daily*), the legacy of Lillie Hitchcock Coit, who left a $125,000 bequest for the purpose of 'adding

One poor couple booked their honeymoon suite 2 years in advance, so they could be sure of spending their wedding night drinking champagne in the jacuzzi. At the last moment they were told that their room had been given to a celebrity. They were so upset, they refused an alternative room offered by the hotel and spent the first night of their honeymoon sleeping on the bride's mother's sitting-room floor. The celebrity was unaware of the mix up, and later said she would happily have moved to another room.

beauty to the city I have always loved'. It also has a memorial to the volunteer firemen who doused the flames of 1906. Take a ride to the top of the tower for some more rewarding views of the city.

For a taste of San Francisco's more sombre past, **Alcatraz**, a mile from the northern waterfront (*ferries from Pier 43, Fisherman's Wharf*), is the formidable-looking island prison that once held Al Capone, and featured in the 1979 Clint Eastwood movie *Escape from Alcatraz*. The concrete cell blocks stand on a craggy island that rises 135ft out of the wild tides of San Francisco Bay.

Fisherman's Wharf, with its fast-food stands, refurbished piers and souvenir shops, is so touristy and crowded that it is hard to believe it was once a working fishing port. Good local **beaches** can be found fronting the **Golden Gate National Recreation Area**, including Baker and China beaches, both just west of Golden Gate Bridge. Baker can be reached by a clearly marked road turning west off Lincoln Boulevard, and the sandy China Beach, from 28th Avenue and Sea Cliff. **Windsurfing** is good around **Berkeley Marina**, a man-made peninsula at the foot of University Avenue. Sailboats can be rented for **cruising** the Bay.

There are numerous **organised sightseeing tours** of the city. Well established is the Grey Line Inc., ✆ (415) 558 9400, which covers the Bay area, including Alcatraz, Sausalito, San Francisco by night, Carmel and the wine country.

Eating Out

Chinatown has many authentic restaurants serving good affordable Chinese food: **Empress of China**, China Trade Center Building, 838 Grant Avenue, ✆ (415) 434 1345 (*moderate*), serves delicious food in elegant surroundings with good views from the top floor. Booking is essential.

Scott's Seafood Grill, 2400 Lombard Street, ✆ (415) 563 8988 (*moderate–inexpensive*), is a very popular, no-nonsense fish restaurant. No reservations can be made—be prepared to queue.

Cathay House, 718 California Street, ✆ (415) 982 3388 (*inexpensive*), is one of Chinatown's best known restaurants.

The Top of the Mark bar, The Mark Hopkins Inter-Continental, 999 California Street, ✆ (415) 392 3434, is a lively cocktail bar for a vodka with a view.

Many hotels serve a good-value brunch at weekends, with an all-in price that includes champagne.

Hotels Nearby

★★★★★**The Ritz–Carlton**, 600 Stockton at California Street, San Francisco, CA 94108, USA, ✆ (415) 296 7465 (*expensive*). Located on the top of Nob Hill, this handsome neoclassical building has comfortable and luxurious rooms.

Queen Anne, 1590 Sutter Street, ✆ (415) 441 2828 (*expensive–moderate*), is an award-winning Victorian guest house filled with antiques, once a girls' boarding school, located in Van Ness district.

Sherman House, 2160 Green Street, ✆ (415) 563 3600 (*moderate*), is a small 'boutique hotel' in Pacific Heights, with canopied feather beds and wood-burning fireplaces.

Checklist

when to go

The **summer** is the best time to visit; temperatures climb into the seventies and invigorating breezes make sightseeing a comfortably non-sticky experience. June is party month, with numerous street fairs and the popular festival on Oakland's Lake Merritt. Recommended are the North Beach Fair, the Haight Street Fair, the Union Street Festival of Arts and Crafts and the Mardi Gras-style carnival in the mission district. Contact the San Francisco Visitor Information Center for more details, ✆ (415) 391 2000.

getting there

By air: A number of carriers offer non-stop or one-stop flights from London to San Francisco. They include: American Airlines, British Airways, Delta and Northwest. San Francisco International Airport is served by nearly all major national and international carriers in the US.

By rail: Amtrak runs daily trains on interstate routes from San Francisco and Los Angeles, also connecting with the Pacific Northwest, Chicago, Las Vegas and New Orleans. Rail services end at Oakland (16th Street Station—a bus transfers passengers to the Transbay Terminal at 1st and Mission streets), ✆ (800) 872 7245.

By car: Five major interstate freeways connect California with points south, east and north.

tour operators

Fly–drive packages, with or without accommodation, are available through tour operators like **Virgin Holidays**, The Galleria, Station Hill, Crawley RH10 1WW, ✆ (01293) 617181, and **British Airways Holidays**, Astral Towers, Betts Way, London Road, Crawley RH10 2XA, ✆ (01293) 617000.

booking direct

There are direct reservation lines in the USA, ✆ (800) 622 0404. Moderately priced special-break honeymoon packages are available. Reservations can also be made through **The Leading Hotels of the World**: from the UK, freefone ✆ (0800) 181 123; from the USA, toll-free ✆ (800) 223 6800.

entry formalities

For stays of 90 days or less, British citizens no longer need a visa to enter the United States. Citizens from all other countries, including Ireland, still need to get a visa before leaving.

getting around

Cable cars are a fun way of getting around. They run on 3 routes throughout the city; day passes are available.

getting by

US dollars, travellers' cheques and major credit cards are accepted.

Love in a Strange Climate 158
How and Where to Wed 159

Alternative Weddings

Wacky Weddings 160
What to Wear 161
Specialist Tour Operators with
  Wedding/Honeymoon Co-ordinators 162
Original Options in the UK 162

The average traditional wedding in the UK costs in the region of £10,000, and in New York many couples spend sums close to $20,000 on the reception. So choosing to tie the knot somewhere other than the local church or register office, even at the honeymoon destination, may be the logical alternative. Weddings away from home have increased tremendously in popularity over the last decade: for example, in 1994 around 12,000 Britons married overseas, 2000 on the island of St Lucia alone.

Love in a Strange Climate

Although the idea of saying 'I will' under a palm tree may sound the ultimate in exotic gestures, the actual event can be hugely disappointing. Beachside weddings have become such big business that many of the most popular holiday islands in the Caribbean are guilty of putting couples through their paces with distinctly unromantic conveyor-belt speed. Brides in billowing white and over-hot grooms dressed in tails frequently find themselves caught in a traffic jam of twosomes while awaiting their turn at the wedding bower. Ironically, this is precisely the kind of treatment that wouldn't have been tolerated by the couple had they opted for the seemingly lacklustre alternative of a home-based ceremony.

Even so, the trade in importing singles and exporting couples looks set to stay. There are strong financial considerations (some resort hotels or specialist tour operators now offer 'free' wedding packages, thrown in for the price of a two-week honeymoon). And getting married abroad can represent a marvellous way of evading unruly uncles and awkward aunts—although operators are increasingly offering a special discount for group bookings of family and friends travelling to attend a wedding, the cost will probably still be high enough to deter casual acquaintances and distant family members. Equally, for second and subsequent marriages, the 'exotic wedding' holds obvious appeal—it's quick, cheap, and at a more attractive venue than the local register office back home. There is also the bonus of avoiding potentially disconcerting feelings of *déjà-vu*.

Top ten wedding destinations

1. St Lucia
2. Kenya
3. Mauritius
4. Seychelles
5. Barbados
6. Bali
7. Thailand
8. Jamaica
9. Florida
10. Fiji

How and Where to Wed

Many established travel agents or tour operators now have specialist wedding co-ordinators—but you can of course organise the event yourselves. The main advantage of doing so is that you avoid the 'packaged' scenario. As well as lining couples up in conveyor-belt fashion, the worst off-the-shelf wedding packages include hazy and expensive photographs, sweet fizzy wine purporting to be champagne, wilting floral bowers and incomprehensible registrars. Going solo means you don't have to put up with hotel guests in swimsuits gawping at you while you exchange your vows, you can say no to the bellhop acting as best man, you can even find a local pastor or priest to conduct your ceremony in a pretty local church.

The disadvantage of organising your own wedding is the paperwork. There is, for example, the complicated business of residency laws. For the Caribbean, residency rules vary from island to island but rarely stipulate a wait of more than a week; in Las Vegas you can marry at any time of the day or night, and you don't even have to stay in town before or afterwards; whereas if you choose parts of Europe you are likely to get embroiled in tedious red tape. Time and perseverence are necessary to decipher the European legal requirements (Italophiles be warned), so start your research weeks before you travel, by telephoning the embassy of your chosen destination.

For other popular wedding destinations around the Indian Ocean—on the Kenyan coast, or on outlying islands like the Seychelles, Mauritius, or Bali—residency requirements tend to be longer. In the Seychelles, couples must normally be 'resident' for 11 days before the wedding, and Bali requires a 7-day residency, with a night in Jakarta to deal with the paperwork.

When all's said and done, specialist tour operators are dab hands at handling all the necessary documentation. Ideally, you should appoint them to deal with the legal side of things, while insisting on your exact requirements with regard to the ceremony itself. You will pay for their time and effort, but it should be worth it.

Key questions to ask a tour operator

- Is there a private corner of the beach or hotel where we can marry? Can we choose our own venue?

- Is a church/synagogue/mosque ceremony possible?

- Can we organise our own flowers and wedding breakfast menu?

- Can we see examples of photographs by the appointed photographer?

Documents needed

To marry abroad you will generally need these documents:

- ✔ Passports
- ✔ Birth certificates
- ✔ If it is not your first marriage, a copy of the Decree Absolute; if you are widowed, proof of your widowhood.

If these are posted in advance, it will speed the procedure up. Again, a specialist co-ordinator should ensure they reach the correct office at the other end. The originals will be needed once you arrive.

Wacky Weddings

Why stick to beaches and palms trees? In **Las Vegas**, famed for 24-hour 'quickie' weddings, choices include drive-in chapels where the ceremony takes 3 minutes and you don't even have to turn the car engine off, to themed ceremonies like the 'Elvis Experience', during which a Presley lookalike serenades the newlyweds then escorts them around town in his pink Cadillac. Wedding chapels are abundant, tiny and tacky: most are resplendently adorned with neon-lit hearts, ornate plasterwork, ribbons, bows and plastic flowers.

At the Excalibur Hotel and Casino, you can get spliced by a priest dressed up as Friar Tuck, and eat Chicken Guinevere afterwards. Or why not opt for the Little White Chapel in the Sky—a giant hot-air 'love balloon' that floats across the Nevada desert? All you need for a Las Vegas 'do' is your passport and $45 for the paperwork. Get your licence from the county clerk's office at the courthouse (on South 3rd Street) and then choose your chapel.

Or why not try an underwater wedding? In **Florida**, keen divers can mouth 'I will' in the company of angel fish, grouper and coral fronds. Satin and

> Las Vegas 'wedding queen' Charlotte Richards, an ordained minister who owns the most famous wedding chapels of Tinsel Town, can offer just about anything in the way of bizarre ceremonies. She has officiated at weddings on horseback, while a bride-to-be was in labour with her first child, and even on top of a mountain where the lovers, extended on ropes, felt they had found the best way of tying the knot. By contrast, there was a couple who rode the Wet'n'Wild rapids while Charlotte performed the ceremony. And she will even marry your pets for you...

Alternative Weddings

Beware, though. Esoteric is fun, but you may end up paying the price for your eccentric tastes. Paula and Bob from Wyoming chose to tie the knot in a hot-air balloon over Florida. Everything went fine—they exchanged their vows at dawn with the balloon wafting over some dramatic landscape...but the 'earth moved' in more ways than one. A high wind forced an early landing, miles from the champagne picnic spot chosen by the couple. Paula fell on top of the registrar, crushed her bouquet, and toppled out of the balloon with much of her expensive lacy lingerie and taffeta gown ending up torn and dirt-covered.

lace wetsuits might be hard to track down, but a tick on a slate will confirm you as man and wife. Virgin Holidays, ✆ (01293) 617181, will do the honours.

In **Orlando**, Disney fans can hire Cinderella's shimmering glass wedding coach pulled by six white ponies, with Mickey Mouse in attendance, ✆ Disney World, (407) 363 6333; and Virgin Holidays, famed for their hot-air balloon ceremonies, have recently introduced 'Heli' Weddings, where couples can plight their troth 8000 feet above Orlando's Lakeland. Down-to-earth lovers may prefer the back of a limousine for the ceremony—or, for the active, a wedding on the ski slopes is possible in **Vermont**, **Nevada** and **Colorado**.

Tropical Places, ✆ (01342) 825599, can offer a Swahili sailing dhow in **Mombasa Creek**, or a game reserve with elephants as wedding guests. If **Thailand** appeals, they can organise a traditional wedding, complete with authentic Thai costumes, attendant Buddhist monks and the skills of a fortune teller.

The fantastical Oriental-rococo Royal Pavilion in **Brighton**, ✆ (01273) 603005, was recently awarded Approved Marriage Status. Ceremonies are conducted in the elegant Red Drawing Room.

In **New York**, take a trip to the top floor of the Empire State Building, ✆ (212) 736 3100, and follow in the footsteps of *Sleepless in Seattle* stars Meg Ryan and Tom Hanks—providing of course, you don't suffer from vertigo.

What to Wear

Taffeta, tulle, satin and net don't travel well. Even if you feel like trusting those creases to the hotel laundry room, the traditional white bridal 'meringue' is not always the ideal choice for a tropical wedding. But if you are desperate for the 'white wedding' look, then check out the local weather temperatures before you decide on your outfit and get the dress adapted accordingly. Cotton is cooler than satin, petticoats make you perspire, but a long lacy veil will at least conceal an overheated complexion!

Beach and island ceremonies are usually quite informal, so what you wear is entirely up to you. For men, light-coloured cotton trousers and a cotton or linen jacket will look more appropriate and feel more comfortable than a topper and tails. A simple silk shift dress for women can be enhanced with accessories such as local tropical flowers in bouquet and hair. You could even play it minimalist with a tiny two-piece.

The more exotic the location, the more likely you are to be able to hire local costumes. If you don't mind living with the photographs, you can opt for grass skirts in the South Pacific, heavily embroidered shifts in Thailand—even Mickey and Minnie Mouse costumes in Florida. If in doubt, go for simplicity and subtlety.

Specialist Operators with Wedding and Honeymoon Co-ordinators

UK

Virgin Holidays, ✆ (01293) 617181
Caribbean Connection, ✆ (01244) 341131
Caribtours, ✆ (0171) 581 3517
Airtours, ✆ (01706) 830130

USA

American Express Vacations, toll-free ✆ (800) 241 1700
GoGo Tours, toll-free ✆ (800) 526 0405
Travel Impressions, toll-free ✆ (800) 284 0044

Original Options in the UK

In Britain, since the Marriage Act of 1994 received royal assent, couples can marry where they please. Local authorities are now empowered to license suitable buildings for the ceremony. The proviso is that the venue should 'not diminish the dignity of marriage' in any way—so beaches, motorways, the back of a fast car and the Big Dipper are out. Even so, English couples can at least now mirror their American and Scottish cousins and marry in pretty gardens, medieval castles, stately homes and Grecian follies. Surprisingly, daily rentals for buildings of historic interest compare favourably to the cost of erecting a huge traditional marquee in the parents' back garden. If you want to find out more information, the Registrar General and each local authority will hold a list of approved premises for weddings, as well as fees charged.

Sporty Honeymoons	164
Big Adventure Honeymoons	165

Alternative Honeymoons

Spiritual Honeymoons	166
Budget Honeymoons	166

If a two-week package on a tropical beach doesn't appeal, then perhaps you should consider a honeymoon that is tailor-made to your tastes. You may, for example, want to settle for the cheaper self-catering option—but in somewhere special like a Gothic folly. Perhaps you like the idea of touring California on a Harley Davidson, or maybe you prefer the thought of visiting a New Age spiritual shrine to a sybaritic escape. Bizarre though your preferences may seem to others, it is a fortunate fact that many tour operators are now catering for even the most esoteric of inclinations. The following suggestions are intended as an 'ideas' guide only; for more comprehensive help it pays to find good specialist tour operators with a working knowledge of the destinations covered by their business. Independent tour operators in particular, for instance those who come under the umbrella of the Association of Independent Tour Operators (AITO) in the UK, offer a huge choice of unusual and affordable holidays. For brochures call ✆ (0891) 515948; from the USA ✆ (0181) 744 318.

Sporty Honeymoons

riding and trekking

Boojum Expeditions, 2625 Garnet Avenue, San Diego, California 92109, ✆ (619) 581 3301, arrange rides through China, Tibet and Inner Mongolia.

Explore Worldwide Ltd, 1 Frederick Street, Aldershot, Hants GU11 1LQ, ✆ (01252) 344161, offer pony-trekking in Kashmir.

Equitour/Peregrine Holidays, 40/41 South Parade, Summertown, Oxford OX2 7JP, ✆ (01865) 511642, arrange treks in Europe, Tanzania, Botswana, Argentina, Belize and Egypt.

skiing

Orient-Express Hotels, toll-free ✆ (800) 237 1236, provide romantic skiing stays at The Lodge at Vail, from the USA. This is just one possibility for skiing fanatics, who should also consider Colorado, Vermont and Nevada—especially if they want to tie the knot on the slopes.

Virgin Holidays, The Galleria, Station Road, Crawley, West Sussex RH10 1WW, ✆ (01293) 617181, can also arrange wedding and honeymoon packages at these destinations.

Argo Holidays, 100 Wigmore Street, London W1H 9DR, ✆ (0171) 331 7070. Greece doesn't spring to mind as a skiing centre, but on Mount Parnassos you find crowd-free pistes as well as plenty of snow. Argo tailor-make two-centre honeymoons combining a few days' skiing on Mount Parnassos with a sun-drenched stay at unspoilt Pelion, the legendary home of the Centaurs and the reputed wedding altar of the Greek gods.

water sports

American Round-up, Oxenways, Membury, Axminster, Devon EX13 7JR, ✆ (01404) 881777. Water-based honeymoons can be more adventurous than a gentle dip in the Caribbean. This is a company that specializes in tailor-made ranch and river-rafting trips in the USA and Canada. Choose from genuine working ranches to luxury ranch resorts, as well as the wilderness adventure of white-water expeditions.

Journey Latin America Ltd, 14–16 Devonshire Road, Chiswick, London W4 2HD, ✆ (0181) 747 8315, offer honeymoon cruises down the Amazon.

The Moorings, in the UK, 188 Northdown Road, Cliftonville, Kent CT9 2QN, ✆ (01843) 227140; in the US, 19345 US 19 North, Suite 402, Clearwater, Florida 34624-3193, ✆ (800) 535 7289. For sailing and big game fishing in the Bahamas, the Seychelles, the Caribbean and Fiji, international charter companies like The Moorings can advise on comfortable and affordable yachts.

Big Adventure Honeymoons

Discover the World Ltd, The Flatt Lodge, Bewcastle, Cumbria CA6 6PH, ✆ (016977) 48361. Choose between wolf- and bear-watching in the Carpathian Mountains.

One groom was a keen golfer and his fiancée had just started taking lessons, so a fortnight in Thailand, with one week on the beach followed by a week on the golf course, seemed ideal. 'When we were on the beach everything was lovely,' recalls the bride. 'But as soon as we started playing golf it became a nightmare. We'd never played together before and he got irritated because I was so slow. After the first day we were barely speaking to each other. Fortunately by the end of the week we'd made it up, so we went out for a final round together. His putting was terrible that day and mine, for once, was great. By some fluke I ended up beating him—which he hated so much that he sulked all the way home. I'd never seen his competitive streak before, and I decided that, for the sake of our marriage, I'd better just give up golf.'

Silverbird, 94 Northfields Prospect, Putney Bridge Road, London SW18 1PE, ✆ (0181) 875 9090. Go junk-cruising in the Far East.

Londozi Game Reserve, reservations PO Box 1211, Sunninghill Park 2157, Republic of South Africa, ✆ (011) 803 8421. If you like your **safaris** with soft beds, champagne, gourmet cooking and hot baths (and on your honeymoon, why not?) try the Eastern Transvaal. A number of luxurious private game reserves have sprung up on the western edges of the famous Kruger National Park, some with their own swimming pools, and dining rooms constructed from balconies suspended 70 feet up in an ebony tree. Daily leopard sightings are virtually guaranteed at the Londozi.

Jetsave Travel Ltd, Sussex House, London Road, East Grinstead, West Sussex RH19 1LD, ✆ (01342) 312033, can arrange for honeymooners to tour Florida on a Harley Davidson. Electra Glide hire is available by the day, including protective clothing and insurance.

Spiritual Honeymoons

Tangney Tours, Pilgrim House, Station Court, Borough Green, Kent TN15 8AF, ✆ (01732) 886666, arrange pilgrimages to Santiago de Compostela, Rome, the Holy Land and Lourdes.

Discover the World (*see above*) organise blue whale watching in California, and swimming with dolphins in Gibraltar.

Nomadic Thoughts, 23 Hopefield Avenue, London NW6 6LJ, ✆ (0181) 960 1001, will tailor-make itineraries to Tibet for the Hottest Retreat treat—an ashram. You could also tour the **temples** of Bali (*see* pp.19–28).

Budget Honeymoons

Affordable **Caribbean** honeymoons are entirely possible if you travel out of season. Low-priced packages in top-class hotels can save almost half what is charged in December—and the climate (bar the hurricane months of July to September), is pretty much the same as in high season. Likewise self-catering, guest houses and traditional inns represent affordable options at any time of the year.

When they married nearly 20 years ago, one couple was so hard up that a honeymoon seemed out of the question—until the bride heard a programme on the radio. As a result they spent their honeymoon at a medical centre where research was being carried out on the common cold virus. 'It was quite comfortable, really,' recalls the groom. 'We had a room to ourselves, lovely countryside around us, and all our meals provided. And only one of us caught the cold.' His bride—the one who was ill—has rather less pleasant memories...

self-catering in the UK

Distinctly Different Holidays, ✆ (01225) 866842, have small, eccentric and well-priced properties. Choose between the Severn Trow, an old brothel on the banks of the River Severn, resplendent with four-poster beds, or Bradford Old Windmill in Bradford-on-Avon. It has circular rooms with king-sized round beds or waterbeds, and there is also a minstrels' gallery.

The National Trust, booking office, ✆ (01225) 791199, has highly individual self-catering properties, including stately home apartments and estate workers' cottages. Romantic retreats include the Birdcage, a tiny five-sided cottage for two in the Cornish fishing village of Port Isaac, and New and Ferry cottages, both of which stand on the banks of the Thames, in the 375 acres of Lord Astor's former garden in Cliveden. The cottages have their own landing stages and rowing dinghies—book early.

The Landmark Trust, for a brochure call ✆ (01628) 825925. Choose from a wonderful selection of lighthouses, Gothic follies, a neoclassical pigsty converted into a cottage for two, railway stations and medieval chapels. All the properties are affordable and furnished with period antiques, good books, local maps and guides to the area. And for a special first night, why not sleep at Hampton Court Palace? You can rent a cosy apartment where the Officers of the Pastry once slept, deep within the the labyrinth of Henry VIII's Tudor Kitchens, known as Fish Court. Landmark Trust handle all bookings.

self-catering in Europe

Venetian Apartments, ✆ (0181) 878 1130. **Venice** is renowned as a romantic destination—and for an authentically seductive base, why not rent a *palazzo* which once belonged to Casanova? Heaps cheaper than a grand hotel, the apartment is wonderfully redolent of passionate trysts. Venetian Apartments have a selection of grand palaces for hire.

Secret Spain, Model Farm, Hightown Green, Rattlesden, Bury St Edmunds, Suffolk IP30 0SY, ✆ (01449) 736096, has traditional characterful houses to let and small charming hotels in undiscovered Northern Spain.

CV Travel's Mediterranean World, 43 Cadogan Street, London SW3 2PR, ✆ (0171) 581 0851, has elegant villas in the Mediterranean, which are still cheaper than grand hotels.

Allez France Holidays Ltd., 27–29 West Street, Storrington, West Sussex RH20 4DZ, ✆ (01903) 742345. In France, luxury **mobile homes** are as comfortable as good hotels but less than half the cost. Located on three- or four-star coastal campsites, they have pools, restaurants and sports facilities.

bed-and-breakfast

Gleneagles Hotel, ✆ (01764) 662231; from the USA, call Crown International, toll-free ✆ (800) 628 8929. Gleneagles, the luxury hotel in the heat of Perthshire, has selected some attractive properties for superior Scottish bed-and-breakfasts. They range from a large Scottish country house on a loch to a charming small country cottage. Book a Gleneagles Bed-and-Breakfast Tour of Scotland, and you can combine these properties with two nights of reasonably priced luxury at Gleneagles itself.

Architectural Holidays, a US-based tour operator, ✆ (203) 431 1350, organise packages to some of Britain's finest castles, where accommodation is in romantic private chambers and castellated turrets. The honeymoon package includes nightly feasts in magnificent great halls, and tailor-made itineraries to a number of enchanting historic sites throughout the UK.

cycling honeymoons

Alternative Travel Group—Fresco Cycling, 69–71 Banbury Road, Oxford OX2 6PE, ✆ (01865) 310399. Tandems may be in short supply, but biking enthusiasts can **cycle** through Italy and France with tailor-made itineraries and budgets to suit all pockets, from £38 a day including accommodation, to deluxe.

Becks Bicycle Tours, 17 High Street, Redbourn, Herts AL3 7LE, ✆ (01582) 793249, can help you head somewhere more esoteric like Bavaria, the Franken Wine Region and parts of the Romantic Road.

La Bicyclette Gourmande, ✆ (89) 49 28 67, combines the joys of riding through lovely countryside with food prepared at the best Gault Millau- and Michelin-commended restaurants in Alsace, just to prove that cycling honeymoons needn't scrimp on those special touches. A 4–7-day tour of the vineyards and countryside costs from 3370FF.

The Cadogan Guides Series

'Cadogan Guides have a reputation as the outstanding series for the independent traveller who doesn't want to follow the crowd...'

Daily Telegraph

'The quality of writing in this British series is exceptional... The Cadogan Guides can be counted on for interesting detail and informed recommendations.'

Going Places

'The characteristic of all these guides is a heady mix of the eminently practical, a stimulating description of the potentially already familiar, and an astonishing quantity of things we'd never thought of, let alone seen.'

The Art Quarterly

'Cadogan Guides are entertaining... They go a little deeper than most guides, and the balance of infectious enthusiasm and solid practicality should appeal to first-timers and experienced travellers alike.'

Michael Palin

'...the guidebooks that are widely acclaimed for their wit, originality and revealing insights.'

Sunday Telegraph

'...proper companions...amusingly written with fascinating snippets on history and culture.'

Woman magazine

'Perhaps the nicest thing about these Cadogan Guides is that they are very informal and relaxed. They strike a happy balance between background and sightseeing information, plus lots of helpful historical notes and amusing anecdotes.'

The Good Book Guide

The Cadogan Guides Series: Other Titles

Country Guides

THE CARIBBEAN & THE BAHAMAS
CENTRAL AMERICA
CENTRAL ASIA
ECUADOR, THE GALAPAGOS & COLOMBIA
EGYPT
FRANCE: THE SOUTH OF FRANCE
FRANCE: SOUTHWEST FRANCE; Dordogne, Lot & Bordeaux
GERMANY
GERMANY: BAVARIA
GOA
GUATEMALA & BELIZE
INDIA
INDIA: SOUTH INDIA
IRELAND
IRELAND: SOUTHWEST IRELAND
IRELAND: NORTHERN IRELAND
ITALY
ITALY: NORTHWEST ITALY
ITALY: SOUTH ITALY
ITALY: THE BAY OF NAPLES & THE AMALFI COAST
ITALY: LOMBARDY, Milan & the Italian Lakes
ITALY: TUSCANY, UMBRIA & THE MARCHES
JAPAN
MEXICO
MOROCCO
PORTUGAL
SCOTLAND
SCOTLAND'S HIGHLANDS & ISLANDS
SOUTH AFRICA
SPAIN
SPAIN: SOUTHERN SPAIN
SYRIA & LEBANON
TUNISIA
TURKEY
TURKEY: WESTERN TURKEY

Also Available

HEALTHY TRAVEL: BUGS BITES & BOWELS
TRAVEL BY CARGO SHIP
FIVE MINUTES OFF THE MOTORWAY

City Guides

AMSTERDAM
BERLIN
BRUSSELS, BRUGES, GHENT & ANTWERP
FLORENCE, SIENA, PISA & LUCCA
LONDON
MOSCOW & ST PETERSBURG
NEW YORK
PARIS
PRAGUE
ROME
VENICE & THE VENETO

Island Guides

BALI
THE CARIBBEAN: N. E. CARIBBEAN The Leeward Islands
THE CARIBBEAN: S. E. CARIBBEAN The Windward Islands
CYPRUS
GREEK ISLANDS
GREECE: THE CYCLADES
GREECE: THE DODECANESE
GREECE: THE IONIAN ISLANDS
MALTA, COMINO & GOZO
SICILY